KAY N. SANECKI

Discovering
Gardens
in Britain

SHIRE PUBLICATIONS LTD

Contents

ACKNOWLEDGEMENTS
  Photographs are acknowledged as follows: Cadbury Lamb, plates 1, 2, 3, 5, 6, 7, 10, 11, 12, 13, 14, 15, 18, 21, 22, 23, 26; The Iris Hardwick Library of Photographs, plates 4, 8, 16, 17, 19, 20, 24, 27; Hazel Le Rougetel, plate 9; Gardening Centre, London, plate 25.
  The line drawings are by Edward Stamp.
  The cover photograph of Hidcote Manor garden, Gloucestershire, is from the Iris Hardwick Library of Photographs.

Printed in Great Britain by C. I. Thomas & Sons (Haverfordwest) Ltd., Merlins Bridge, Haverfordwest.

Introduction

The discovery of gardens is the discovery of pleasure. It comes not only in the personal enjoyment gained from visiting gardens but in the reflection that since the Renaissance 'pleasure gardens' have been part of a way of life. The visitor must learn to regard a garden, whatever the size, as an art form — an ongoing piece of work — rather than a practical exercise in gardening. Naturally one muses upon the making of some of the great gardens of the seventeenth and eighteenth centuries, when, without mechanical means, gangs of workers set about making lakes and constructing terraces and courtyards with crude and heavy implements. One must always enter the scene as a whole, absorb the atmosphere and consider the overall design and form, background, reflections, textures, all of which play a part in forming the general picture. The enjoyment is not only visual but is often derived from the interpretation of what is seen. Gardens are like rooms in that they can be an expression of their owner's taste, wealth, interests and even dreams. Often, just as the impact of a room can be immediately attractive, so one can discover a spontaneous sympathy with a garden — and sometimes return again and again to rediscover it as a work of art.

The British have developed a sensitivity towards gardens and regard their own, be it 'pocket handkerchief' or manorial estate, as something highly personal, but they tend to take for granted the provision of gardens for public use. It is now accepted that the public should be given access to many hitherto privately owned gardens. Ownership today, whether by local authority, national organisation, private or civic trust, carries some obligation to open the gates to the public, not for inspection but for enjoyment. Many private owners open their gardens today not for gain, as might be imagined, but in order to maintain the gardens. Several have established successful plant sales counters or even garden centres and nurseries so that the gardens themselves shall not fall into dereliction.

Since the 1930s, and more especially since the Second World War, the contribution made by the National Trust to the maintenance, restoration and renovation of gardens in their care has been remarkable. And while many estates can now be visited and the gardens enjoyed the public has a reciprocal obligation to subscribe to that privilege not only financially but with respect. As gardens are restored, improved or simply saved from the disorder which nature makes when left to her own devices, more people visit them. Unfortunately the increase in the number of garden visitors is proportionate to the increase in damage done to the gardens, and thus the amenity is not only misunderstood but

3

misused. People like to have 'somewhere to go' and set out not knowing what to expect when gardens are visited. The visitor must be made aware of the meaning of gardens (as opposed to gardening) for it is only by increased understanding that he can fully appreciate the surroundings.

A good visitor, like a good driver, expects the unexpected. Gardens are enjoyed for different reasons by different people: to some they provide an opportunity for a walk in pleasant surroundings; to others they are a social history book, a collection of botanical specimens or a lesson in design. An imaginary picture is often formed of a garden about which one has read or heard or even seen photographs but, as soon as one arrives there, all the previous ideas are banished and the atmosphere of the garden speaks for itself. Period will probably hint at what can be expected, as will size, soil and aspect. The larger gardens become known as a water garden, a woodland garden or a formal garden, but all these are comprehensive names. Frequently the general guides to gardens open to the public label a garden in this way and the visitor finds so much more of charm and interest than the autumn colour or fountains and garden buildings he has been briefed to expect. It is from the interpretation of the various features that make garden design that most enjoyment is to be derived. No one can hope to understand everything in a season or two of garden visiting and discovery is never complete but is a continual pleasure. The individual plants and planting schemes are there for the benefit of the connoisseur and to delight the eye or suggest new ideas to the amateur; getting to know plants is another subject in itself. But the colour and texture and type of plant is the fabric with which the garden is made and the atmosphere created. Naturally shade-loving woodland plants like primulas, hostas and lilies must not be expected in a garden on a baked chalk hillside, and sub-tropical bedding is not likely to be found on the exposed Pennines.

1. Looking at history

Period is a vague term when applied to gardening: while the original site or part of a site may have been laid down as a garden in a certain period and not redesigned since, it cannot be quite as it was intended to be, because it is a living art form. Frequently more recent plants have been introduced, or the general outline of the garden is all that remains. The unravelling of the story can only be done gradually, starting by reading about the garden, looking at old prints, plans or photographs and then by applying other knowledge about contemporary or more recent garden history.

Each period expressed its tastes and often used the newest ideas or materials in garden making. Features of Elizabethan gardens still to be seen are mounts, gazebos, some water conduits, terracing and walls, but this does not mean that the terracing surrounding every Elizabethan manor or the gazebo across the lawn is necessarily of the same period. The garden visitor has to use a discerning eye and apply all the available information about contemporary and more recent building practice.

The seventeenth century brought a regularity of design in long canals, formally clipped hedges and isolated specimens (topiary) and complex hydraulics. It was an age in which formalism far exceeded its purpose. It was also a great tree-planting era, especially of mighty avenues striking out across the countryside away from the houses and gardens themselves.

Understandably the violent reaction of the landscapists of the eighteenth century sought to sweep away the straight lines mathematically conceived and to emulate the natural features of the countryside. A great breadth of treatment and freedom of design brought the grass up to the windows of the mansion, used trees and water as the sole materials and confined the developing practice of horticulture within the walls of the rectangular kitchen garden. The classical and the aesthetic appeal became paramount but by the closing years of the century and the very early years of the nineteenth a need arose to be a little more decorative and at the same time to use some of the newly introduced plants in the garden scheme.

With the increasing prosperity of the nineteenth century and the ever increasing flow of new and exciting plants the landscape ceased to monopolise gardening efforts and the revival of ambitious patterned planting schemes became inevitable. Victorian formality relied almost exclusively upon the number and the colour contrast of plants and not upon architectural proportions as in previous centuries. This was another age of tree planting, but mainly to establish collections of trees, both deciduous and coniferous, introduced from overseas. Many important collections

5

made at this time exist today. Many public parks date from Victorian times, too; the Crown Estate parks, St James's Park, Hyde Park and Regent's Park in London, had been open to the public for some time but the provision of open spaces for the enjoyment of the new town dwellers dates from this period. There had been public gardens made in Georgian cities, but the first municipal park for the people was Derby Arboretum, today still very much as Loudon designed it.

Also during the nineteenth century a number of private collections of tender plants were assembled in localities where advantage could be taken of the mild climates of south-west England and the western seaboard of Scotland, an effect of the Gulf Stream.

Following the Victorian disregard for the individual beauty and cultural requirement of plants there came a call to use them in a far more natural way and to have confidence in nature. At the same time a plethora of plants was arriving in Europe, notably from China and Tibet and, together with all the new varieties of garden origin, gave impetus to principles of natural gardening. Thus gardeners became initiated into the delights of hardy plant gardening — be it shrub border, rock garden, woodland garden or herbaceous border — which has dominated twentieth-century taste. One aspect that echoes the formality and seclusion of previous centuries is the making of a series of small gardens interconnected to form the whole, a practice of which there are numerous twentieth-century examples.

But although taste and economic prosperity have influenced the pattern of garden making over the centuries, there are many gardens where current fashion was not followed. Herein lies the fascination of garden history and here begins the unravelling and the detective work to expose the form and explore the reasons behind the history of every garden.

2. The fabric of gardens

Walls

The use of walls to provide protection for tender plants is a common horticultural practice and the selection of the aspect, say a south or south-west facing wall, is often crucial for success. Warmth is absorbed during the day from the sunshine and reflected after sunset — a simple fact that is often put to good use to encourage the ripening of fruit. The aspect of the wall is of particular significance because so-called frost damage is really brought about by the morning sunshine reaching frosted growth and speeding the rate of thaw. Thus an east or south-east facing wall would not support tender plants as easily as a south or south-west facing one. The garden visitor, especially the plantsman, can find much of interest among wall-grown shrubs. Sometimes a doubtfully hardy plant for a particular area can be found flourishing happily when grown with wall protection.

Walls may be those of buildings or of former buildings now in ruins, as at Nymans (West Sussex) or Sudeley Castle (Gloucestershire), or walls below terracing as at Powis Castle (Powys) or Cliveden (Buckinghamshire). Low walls are frequent features of many gardens, either as retaining walls for banks or raised beds or for the completion of a terrace. Balustrading, usually of stone but sometimes of lead or iron, decorates these terrace walls and bears a vast assortment of finials and other ornament. Urns, lions, statuary, plant containers of various kinds, lamps, foliage, serpents, little lead gods, horses — all can be found perching on walls. Modern terracing does not seem to require this type of adornment but many of the older gardens, especially those constructed in the nineteenth century on sloping sites, are terraced elaborately. Ornate balustrades and flights of steps, sometimes quite theatrical in proportion, can be seen at such localities as Harewood House (West Yorkshire), Trentham Park (Staffordshire), Chatsworth (Derbyshire), Cliveden and Waddesdon Manor (Buckinghamshire). Often the use of several small steps to change levels, as in modern terracing and patios, is an unobtrusive detail. The use by Sir Edwin Lutyens of changing levels on terraces and paths near the house is particularly interesting; evidence can be perhaps best seen at Hestercombe (Somerset), especially around his orangery. It is the happiest device for relating a building to the site of the surrounding garden.

Walled gardens

Walled gardens proper are a source of endless information to the visitor with an enquiring mind and a little imagination. Materials vary according to the locality, and the design of the coping is sometimes picturesque, as in Dorset and Somerset, where tiles or thatch are set like little eaves along the wall. Walled gardens have existed since medieval times when most of the cultivated land was outside the keep of the homestead; they provided protection against feud, vandals and animals but latterly they served for the extension of horticultural practice. During the eighteenth and nineteenth centuries there was a walled kitchen garden in most large gardens and dozens can still be seen. Few are maintained, though that at Felbrigg Hall (Norfolk) is being refurbished by the National Trust. Some are continued as nurseries, but far too many have fallen into disuse.

Where the garden visitor is allowed access, several points of interest can be searched for. Old fruit trees, no longer trained, may remain, for example pears, and perhaps there may be a vestige of paint, especially on a south or south-west facing wall where protective glass structures have been removed, as at Hutton-in-the-Forest (Cumbria), or evidence of former fruit cases. Good brick paths, well patterned, frequently still form the basis of a rectilinear design of the walled garden. Kitchen garden pathways had to be well made to be functional and to carry the heavy wheelbarrows and water carts of the period. Sometimes old rhubarb or seakale forcing pots are seen, often in disuse, or bell glasses, the forerunners of the modern plastic cloche.

Nowadays the walled garden is not always used for the cultivation of fruit and vegetables and several good examples exist of attractive alternative use. At Mottisfont Abbey (Hampshire) the National Trust is building up a very good collection of old roses within the walled garden. At Wallington (Northumberland) the walled garden is set apart from the house and contains good terracing, attractive planting and a little stream.

Decorative walls

Very occasionally high walls are treated decoratively, echoing days of former opulence, and may have finials or carved coping or the scallop top such as one finds at Alton Towers (Staffordshire). Wall building and bricklaying is prohibitively expensive now but it has been the pastime of some gardeners, notably Sir Winston Churchill, who built the wall of the kitchen garden at his home at Chartwell (Kent). Serpentine or 'crinkle crankle' walls, a fetish of nineteenth-century builders, requiring less material than the solid wall, were built along a wavy line, as at Melford Hall (Suffolk). They were usually of brick and most examples remain in Suffolk, though there is one isolated example in Oxfordshire.

The base of the wall on the sunny side is a very dry spot and for this reason during the eighteenth century it was not uncommon to form a series of arches in the wall in order to plant fruit trees on the north or shaded side and encourage and train their fruiting branches to the warm side of the wall. Remains of fruit arches (now filled in) can be seen clearly at Arbury Hall (Warwickshire).

A further device for simplifying the cultivation of fruit against walls was the practice of heating the wall by means of internal flues. This prevented damage by frost of the blossom and encouraged setting, with subsequent heavier crops. Fires were made in 'ovens' either behind the walls, as can be seen at Parnham House (Dorset), or in the pavilion-like corner buildings at Packwood House (Warwickshire). Another practice to encourage fruiting was to incline brick-faced walls to the sky, as at Biddulph Grange (Staffordshire), and to build up inclined beds against walls to capture more sunshine for the fruiting of strawberries, as in the series of bays at Trengwainton (Cornwall).

Boundary walls

Boundary walls of great length built at considerable cost in the past enclose many estates, some of them with the date of the construction worked into the wall itself as at Hartwell House (Buckinghamshire). Sometimes the wall dominated the village or roadway as at Wilton (Wiltshire), Petworth (West Sussex) and

The Ionic Temple at Duncombe Park, North Yorkshire.

Hatfield House (Hertfordshire). The varying design of gates and gatehouses provides interest, though it is sad to see so many in a state of disrepair. Lodges, quite often in pairs and of remarkably different design, were the homes of gatekeepers, whose duty was to open and close the gates of the estate twenty-four hours a day. The forerunner of the gate with its lodge was the gatehouse and many old ones survive. The loveliest examples are at Lanhydrock (Cornwall), Charlecote Park (Warwickshire), Blenheim Palace (Oxfordshire), Castle Howard (North Yorkshire), Cranborne Manor (Dorset), Mentmore (Buckinghamshire), and Hardwick Hall (Derbyshire). Elsewhere they may be all that remains of a former garden.

Garden buildings

Garden design depends first upon ideas, but the fabric is of the materials, plants and stone. Many kinds of garden buildings are to be seen: some are architectural poems, examples of design uninhibited by functional requirement; others are loggias, pavilions or mere follies. Whatever form they may take, their purpose is to provide a point to which one could walk or a decoration at the culmination of a vista or merely a lavish embellishment to the landscape garden.

Temples

Garden temples were built during the eighteenth and nineteenth centuries, often of classical design and intended as a punctuation mark in the landscape. It has been said that 'temples are trifles and best seen by chance' but they were not constructed as throwaway embellishment. Many were thoughtfully and lavishly decorated and enhanced by statuary or frescoes within. Most frequently to be seen are the mock classical temples raised to the goddesses Diana or Venus or as a *temple d' amour;* the purpose was the same and often they were set in the more remote parts of the garden or estate. Perhaps the best examples are to be seen at Stourhead (Wiltshire), Studley Royal and Castle Howard (North Yorkshire), Hall Barn and West Wycombe Park (Buckinghamshire) and Lee Ford (Devon).

Pavilions and garden houses

Pavilions, usually designed by an architect, differed from temples in that they were more functional. (The ancient concept of a pavilion was as a tent, with its associations of temporary residence.) Sometimes beautifully decorated inside with marble, as at Tyringham (Buckinghamshire), or pleasingly embellished, they were intended as an alternative sitting room for estate entertaining. Food and music could be provided, embroidery and conversation carried on there. The pavilion, designed by Thomas Archer, at the head of the canal at Wrest Park (Bedfordshire) is a particularly good example, and there an upper floor affords a good view of the surrounding garden.

The idea of climbing to a first floor or a raised garden building to gain a prospect was not new to the builders of pavilions. In England in Tudor and Stuart gardens a banqueting house was usually erected on raised ground to afford a wide view, and the mount itself was a device which allowed the occupants of the garden to see what was going on outside. The gazebo, also, was a somewhat frivolous concept of the Elizabethan era — although the word is of more recent usage — and the idea has persisted as a garden building. Its purpose was to allow, from the upper floor, an uninterrupted view of the countryside beyond the confines of the garden, or to overlook an approach carriageway, or to serve as a vantage point above terraces. Remarkably good examples of Elizabethan pavilions of this kind are to be seen at Montacute (Somerset) and Parnham House (Dorset), and there are further examples at Melford Hall (Suffolk), Pitmedden House (Grampian) and Heslington Hall (North Yorkshire).

Garden houses vary widely not only with the period of their construction but with the imagination and requirement of the owners. To call the Praeneste at Rousham, designed by William Kent during the first half of the eighteenth century, a garden house may be considered sacrilegious, but it is strictly a loggia or arcade, open on one side and designed as a garden house. In contrast there are various rustic structures of more recent times, made of wood, thatch, brick or stone and consisting of merely a seat in an alcove or a so-called 'summerhouse' across a lawn. The summerhouse at Spetchley Park (Worcestershire), one of the oldest of its kind, is constructed of roots, tree trunks and thatch. Examples intermediate between the superb Praeneste and the rustic structures of Edwardian rose gardens abound in many gardens in Britain, where when it is not warm enough to sit in the shade a temporary cover is welcome during the showers.

Arbours

The idea of a shelter in the garden has existed for centuries and there are many examples of arches, canopied alcoves and 'little houses'. The most elaborate and noteworthy is that wrought in iron at Melbourne Hall (Derbyshire) and known as the Birdcage Arbour. It was made during the first decade of the eighteenth century by an English blacksmith, Robert Bakewell, who was given a forge on the estate from which to work. Restored to its black and gold splendour, it stands on raised ground beyond the pool, commanding a view of the house and formal garden.

Another fascinating little arbour is the Shell Arbour at Stowe (Buckinghamshire). Here a stone alcove stands beside the path; inside the decoration of pebbles includes animal designs. This arbour was fashioned by William Kent in the eighteenth century

11

and when it was restored in the 1960s and new pebbles were found to replace lost ones the original rough outline of the design was found on the plasterwork.

Living arbours have come to be known as tree houses and are made of yew, as at Antony House (Cornwall) and Great Chalfield Manor (Wiltshire), or of beech, as at Forde Abbey (Dorset) and Ashridge (Hertfordshire). (These ought not to be confused with houses built in trees, 'tree houses' as such. We are told that the King of the Belgians had one in Winter Down Wood, at Claremont, Surrey.) The fashioning of rooms within growing material such as hedges also produces corridors, windows and doorways as are to be seen at Sudeley Castle (Gloucestershire).

Orangeries

Orangeries are frequently very attractive garden buildings, many of them architect designed. They were the precursors of the greenhouse and conservatory. By the end of the seventeenth century the gardens of most large houses had an orangery, which was a building designed to protect orange plants. Tubs were used for the cultivation so that the plants could be grown out of doors in the summer and taken back into the orangery once frost threatened. The orangery was almost always designed as a spacious building roofed like a house with large windows at both sides and at the front. Where heating was provided it came from wood or coal fires, the warmth contained in the back wall or in underground flues. Several excellent examples are to be seen, some renovated, some sadly in a state of neglect. At Ashridge (Hertfordshire) the former orangery is now an integral part of the house, but functional buildings can be seen at Wrest Park (Bedfordshire) — now a restaurant, Sherborne Castle (Dorset), Ammerdown Park and Montacute (Somerset), Saltram House near Plymouth (Devon), Hampton Court, the Royal Botanic Gardens at Kew, Charlecote Park (Warwickshire), Blickling Hall (Norfolk), Powis Castle (Powys) and Bowood (Wiltshire).

The magnificence and adornment of orangeries was a way of displaying the owner's wealth and later the facilities needed for growing other tender and exotic plants were provided as fashion dictated. So the furnishing of conservatories came about. In the eighteenth century splendid glass structures were built, still designed with a solid back wall, but far lighter and often domed. Marvellous structures of this kind are at Bicton Gardens (Devon), Dallam Tower (Cumbria) and Syon Park in west London.

Camellia houses were developed in parallel to orangeries. They were designed with enormous casement windows which could be thrown open during warm weather and were used exclusively for the cultivation of camellias. Their popularity reached its peak in the mid nineteenth century before it was realised that the camellia

Stourhead, Wiltshire.

13

was a perfectly hardy plant in many areas of Britain. At Woburn Abbey (Bedfordshire) camellias can still be seen flowering in such houses early in the year.

Conservatories and greenhouses

The decoration of conservatories with tender plants became very popular at the end of the eighteenth century and continued apace throughout the nineteenth and into the early decades of the twentieth century. Heating such spaces was made easier after the advent of cast-iron water pipes, which provided not only a more even distribution of heat but also a fume-free atmosphere. Cast iron was also the material for narrow girders and glazing bars, so that lighter and more delicate structures became fashionable. Good conservatories, not necessarily maintained in use for plant display, are at Wallington (Northumberland), the Royal Botanic Gardens at Kew, Ashridge (Hertfordshire), Broughton Hall (North Yorkshire), Shrubland Park (Suffolk), Tatton Park (Cheshire), Arlington Court (Devon) and Alveston, Hampshire.

During the nineteenth century the plants used to decorate a conservatory, which had generally become an adjunct of the house, were customarily raised in a greenhouse. Greenhouses were also the factories producing the thousands of plants required to meet the demand for the Victorian summer bedding schemes. Old ranges of greenhouses are to be seen today, most of them sadly dilapidated, dangerous and unused, while in the nineteenth century they were virtually the hub of the garden.

Modern greenhouses are mostly confined to the botanic gardens and training centres. At the Royal Botanic Garden, Edinburgh, a superstructure of steel cables supports the glass from the outside, leaving the interior free of girders. A similar but simpler design has been carried out on the glasshouses at Chatsworth (Derbyshire). It is fitting that the great estate of Chatsworth should lead the way, because it was there that Joseph Paxton designed and built a conservatory which was the forerunner of his great construction, the Crystal Palace of 1851.

Details of interest at older plant houses are the floor tiles, the grilles covering the hot-water pipes, water tanks, fenestration, latches and ventilators. Modern glasshouses are fully automated with thermostatically controlled heating and humidity range, so that a wide variety of climatic conditions can be emulated. A good example is found in the new range of glasshouses at the Royal Horticultural Society's garden at Wisley (Surrey), where within a comparatively small area several varying environmental conditions are maintained without constant attention.

Sundials

Formerly known simply as a dial, the sundial has been a feature of gardens since ancient times. Its purpose was to indicate the time of day, and many dials are still set accurately to serve this purpose. They take several forms, but each has a plate or dial and a gnomon or style whose shadow is cast by the sun on to the graduated dial. As garden ornaments sundials are usually of the pedestal type and are frequently used as a focal point on a terrace or as the central feature in a formal garden. Another type is found on walls, often in stable yards or on gatehouses. There is one on the library wall at Queens' College, Cambridge, painted in brilliant colours depicting the signs of the zodiac, and another remarkable one is in the garden of Merton College, Oxford. At Packwood House (Warwickshire) there is a seventeenth-century wall sundial. Another kind of sundial is the facet-headed type or polyhedron, with stone pedestal dials. There is an attractive one of pink stone at Barrington Court (Somerset) and another of seventeenth- and eighteenth-century origin at Penshurst Place (Kent). The former has twenty-two time-telling facets, so that in sunshine several facets may show the time simultaneously.

There are several attempts at making sundials of living material, the most successful being at Ascott (Buckinghamshire), where the gnomon is of yew with a decorative finial of golden yew. The Roman numerals surrounding it are of clipped box and surrounding these, also in clipped box, is the motto 'Light and shade by turn, but love always'.

Mottoes and quotations often seem to accompany sundials when they are set in gardens. Many are classic examples about the fleeting nature of life; others are pure 'God-wottery'. The garden visitor may derive much pleasure from 'collecting' sundials.

Ice houses

The forerunner of the refrigerator, specially constructed in the garden, was the ice house, where snow and ice could be kept for the preservation of food. An underground pit or chamber was required, with easy access so that the ice could be brought in and where drainage could be provided to keep the ice dry. Sometimes a 'house' was constructed above ground and shaded well by trees. The ice house at Holkham Hall (Norfolk) is apart from the house on a small knoll where drainage could be ensured and it has a thatched roof to keep the interior cool. There is another good example at Tapeley Park (Devon), where the construction is an igloo type of building. Ice houses generally fell into disuse during the latter half of the nineteenth century, when ice-making machines became available.

Dovecotes

The word *dove* was formerly applied to all species of pigeons known in Britain, and so it can be said that dovecotes were built to house pigeons. They were sometimes circular buildings, sometimes rectangular, usually isolated in the garden or kitchen garden and

15

intended to provide shelter and nesting places for pigeons. In the seventeenth century it was estimated that there were twenty-six thousand dovecotes in Britain. At that time the pigeon was an important item in the winter diet. Fresh meat was not obtainable, especially towards the end of the winter, because cattle could not be kept other than those for breeding purposes. In about the 1730s 'Turnip' Townsend improved the production of mangolds and turnips, thus providing more winter fodder for the animals, and from the mid eighteenth century pigeon husbandry declined. Comparatively few dovecotes remain, but those acquired by the National Trust have been restored, and several others, notably at Athelhampton (Dorset) and Rousham House (Oxfordshire), have also been refurbished and make most attractive garden buildings.

Inside a dovecote contains hundreds of nesting holes set in rows and built into brick or stone walls, sometimes extending from the eaves almost to ground level, although usually high. The entrance for the birds is usually in the roof, through a dormer or series of dormers or in the cupola, or through a simple hole beneath the roof. The size of the building varies according to the wealth of the original owner or the size of the estate. The older manorial dovecotes are splendid structures.

Regional building materials and styles also vary; timber seems to have been popular in the west country, stone in Dorset, Wiltshire, Oxfordshire, Northamptonshire and Warwickshire, and brick in East Anglia. Dovecotes are not exclusive to gardens, but there are several noteworthy ones in gardens open to the public or in the nearby home farm or village.

At Rousham House there is a small round dovecote in an old-world area of the garden, near the stable yard and now surrounded by roses and clipped box edges. Not far away, at Chastleton House (Oxfordshire), the dovecote is across the road from the house and garden, while at Nymans Garden (West Sussex) it is built into the wall and is surrounded by camellias and magnolias. Other notable examples in gardens open to the public are at Lytes Cary (Somerset), Athelhampton (Dorset), Dunster Priory (Somerset), Cotehele (Cornwall), Compton Wynyates (Warwickshire), Charleston Manor (East Sussex) and at Hodnet Hall (Salop), where the dovecote is away on farmland but has been used as an eye-catcher in the twentieth-century garden.

Aviaries

The keeping of decorative birds such as black swans, as at Chartwell (Kent), Chinese geese, peacocks and guinea fowl is a common practice of ancient standing. Especially during the eighteenth century the keeping of exotic birds and animals in a menagerie was a favourite adjunct to the garden interest. Aviaries are uncommon in Britain today, though one is to be seen at Waddesdon Manor (Buckinghamshire), property of the National

Trust. Here, at one end of a formal rose garden set apart from the house, is a fantastic pavilion-like aviary. Statuary of marble, a fountain and ferns form the central feature, flanked by well maintained trellis cages all painted white. The aviary and its accompanying garden were in a state of devastation when the National Trust took over in the 1960s and now the refurbished garden is adorned with a simple central lawn, edged with the rose 'Iceberg' and surrounded by a white pebble path. The cages are filled with interesting birds and macaws have free range nearby and fly about neighbouring horse-chestnut trees. The Chinese aviary at Dropmore (Buckinghamshire) stretches along a walk. It no longer houses birds, and indeed it is not often to be seen, but it is one of the most magnificent iron structures in the Chinese style in any British garden. The old Ravens' Cage at Regent's Park, London, designed by Decimus Burton in 1827, was a great attraction in its day, but in the 1960s it was superseded by the modern bird house designed by Lord Snowdon.

Bramham Park, West Yorkshire.

17

Statuary

Statuary of varying quality is to be found in many gardens, sometimes badly defaced by the weather or covered in ivy and of little beauty, and sometimes in poor taste. From ancient times collections of statuary have been assembled to adorn gardens and remind man of his deities. It was only when representations of kings, dukes and generals were used that propriety demanded that they be robed.

Wooden statues of the sixteenth century were painted for preservation and when in the eighteenth century figures were made to people the landscape garden they were sometimes painted white to resemble marble and to contrast with the greenery. Some good eighteenth-century work is still to be seen at Rousham House (Oxfordshire), where across the bowling green are two works by Scheemakers, *Lion attacking a Horse* and *Dying Gaul;* both were made after originals in the Capitoline Museum in Rome. Scheemakers worked with Rysbrack on the Temple of British Worthies at Stowe (Buckinghamshire) and is thought to have made the busts. The setting for statues is shared again in London, where in the garden around Lord Burlington's villa, now Chiswick Park, William Kent introduced an exedra — or outdoor area with seats used for conversation. Here one may see work by Rysbrack, Palladio and Inigo Jones in a semicircle together with vases and some other figures brought from Hadrian's villa near Tivoli in Italy.

During the sixteenth and seventeenth centuries Dutch immigrants made statuary near Hyde Park Corner in London, many working in lead. Some of this work may be seen at Stourhead in Wiltshire, where the *River God* by John Cheere is approached through a series of arches to form a grotto at the side of the lake, while the *Nymph of the Grot* slumbers nearby. The lead figures of the period were less classical in approach and numerous playful figures of shepherds and shepherdesses, as at Charlecote Park (Warwickshire), cherubs and putti, gamekeepers, haymakers and other rural figures came to enhance gardens. The work of Jan Van Nost, a Dutch immigrant, is particularly attractive and he used lead to fashion urns and vases of immense size, such as the Vase of the Four Seasons at Melbourne Hall (Derbyshire), made in 1715 at a cost of £100. At Rousham House (Oxfordshire) his copy of the *Medici Venus* stands sentinel over Venus's Vale attended by two lead figures each astride a swan.

Variously attributed to Van Nost or his assistant, Carpentiere, or to John Cheere and others, the superb lead figures that balance along the balustrade at Powis Castle (Powys) provide excellent examples of the style of work which was fashionable at that period.

The use of urns and vases in garden design became increasingly popular during the nineteenth century for several reasons. They

The Temple of British Worthies, Stowe, Buckinghamshire.

were less expensive than figures and less demanding of location because the form remains the same from whichever angle it is viewed, and it provided the Victorians with something with which to fill empty spaces!

Interesting statuary is to be seen at Dartington Hall (Devon) and Newby Hall (North Yorkshire). At Anglesey Abbey (Cambridgeshire) the National Trust has a superb and extensive collection which Lord Fairhaven brought together from 1926 onwards, and work by Van Nost, Rysbrack and John Cheere is to be seen there as well as interesting Coade-stone caryatids (a product of Victorian times). At Iford Manor (Wiltshire) Sir Harold Peto designed the terrace with colonnades to house statuary, some of it his own, and stone urns. At Wilton House (Wiltshire) some of the oldest examples may be found. At Hever Castle (Kent) William Astor has amassed a varied collection, now displayed in bays along a wall. Many public gardens and parks include statuary and ornament of this kind. The well-known fairy-tale figure of Peter Pan in Kensington Gardens, London, was wrought in bronze by George Frampton in 1912 to commemorate J. M. Barrie, the originator of Peter Pan. The work of Barbara Hepworth and Henry Moore is set in sites in several new towns and Henry

Moore's pieces on a turning plinth are increasingly seen, where the play of light enhances the work itself.

Herb gardens

Formal herb gardens have become a popular feature since the Second World War and the Royal Horticultural Society has made an extensive new one at Wisley (Surrey). While herbs are all old-world economic plants, they have never before been grown in so decorative a way as now. Since the eighteenth century they have been kept in the kitchen garden and only such plants as lavender and rosemary used in the decorative garden. Previously such plants as box, santolina, hyssop and thyme were recommended for outlining the intricate and scroll-like designs of the knot gardens, but we have very little evidence that anything else was used.

The National Trust has responded to the present interest in these simple plants and made some good collections, especially at Hardwick Hall (Derbyshire), Little Moreton Hall (Cheshire), Charlecote Park (Warwickshire) — plants known to Shakespeare, and Acorn Bank (Cumbria). Good herb gardens, all planned on formal lines, are to be seen at Sissinghurst Castle (Kent), where Vita Sackville-West made a herb garden during the Second World War, the paths being laid in 1937, at Hever Castle and Wye College (Kent), Longstock Park (Hampshire), Gaulden Manor (Somerset), Liverpool University Botanic Garden at Ness (Cheshire), Hall Place, Bexley (London) and Cranborne Manor (Dorset). Numerous small corners and borders where representative collections have been assembled are to be found, especially in private gardens.

Water

Water is found in many gardens of all periods, whatever the scale and design. It may be used either still and calm, when it reflects the sky and colour and adds to the expanse of the garden, or splashing and wandering along to provide movement, gaiety and sound. Smooth areas of water, formal or informal in shape, always emphasise the quietness of a garden. Informal lakes are to be seen in many places, notably at Sheffield Park (East Sussex), Stourhead (Wiltshire) and Blenheim Palace (Oxfordshire). Cascades, waterfalls and streams dancing about are notable at Wisley (Surrey), Hodnet Hall (Salop), the Showerings Garden (Somerset) and Cotehele House (Cornwall). Water can be used in a formal concept to emphasise design as at Buscot Park (Oxfordshire), Chatsworth House (Derbyshire), Westbury Court (Gloucestershire) and Wrest Park (Bedfordshire) and in such cases is usually referred to as a canal. There is a remarkable water parterre in a somewhat exuberant manner at Blenheim Palace (Oxfordshire). Moats of medieval homesteads survive and are sometimes incorporated in the garden design of today, sometimes as a dry ditch as at Blickling Hall (Norfolk) or as a water feature as at Compton Wynyates (Warwickshire), Hever Castle (Kent) and at Broughton Castle (Oxfordshire).

Monastic sites, which were the first ever to be 'gardened', were often associated with a river; many remain as gardens bordering a river as at Bisham Abbey (Berkshire), the Temple Gardens and Westminster Abbey Gardens in London and Fountains Abbey (North Yorkshire), now part of the grounds of Studley Royal. The incorporation of a river into the garden scene adds an air of permanence, whether it be a distant view or borrowed landscape, as at Cliveden (Buckinghamshire), Charlecote Park (Warwickshire) or Rousham House (Oxfordshire), or as part of the garden itself, as at Wilton House (Wiltshire), Clare College (Cambridge), Chiswick Park (London), Cranborne Manor (Dorset), the Royal Botanic Gardens at Kew and Syon House (London), Mottisfont Abbey (Hampshire) and Levens Hall Park (Cumbria).

The remains of bath houses are to be seen occasionally and always arouse much curiosity and not a little astonishment that earlier generations should have bathed out of doors. Forerunners of the vogue for swimming pools in the garden, bath houses provided for splashing about (but not swimming) in cold water. The remains of such pools are to be seen at Wrest Park (Bedfordshire) and at Corsham Court (Wiltshire).

A variety of design is to be found in bridges of stone or wood, but the three most noteworthy are the Palladian bridges at Wilton House (Wiltshire), Stowe (Buckinghamshire) and Prior Park

The Palladian Bridge, Wilton House, Wiltshire.

21

(Avon). Palladianism is an architectural style which crept into landscape adornment at the time of William Kent, and apart from the house at Holkham Hall (Norfolk) it is evident at Rousham House (Oxfordshire), where Kent built the seven-arched Praeneste arcade in the Palladian style. Decorative bridges are quite popular but add mainly to garden design at Pusey House (Oxfordshire), Stourhead (Wiltshire), Sezincote (Gloucestershire) and Shugborough (Staffordshire).

Fountains, on the other hand, are features in which water is contrived to spurt forth, not only to add movement and sound to the garden but also a considerable amount of reflected light. In England during the eighteenth century fountains were a rarity in gardens; perhaps the only notable one to be built was at Holkham Hall, Norfolk.

Rather, it was the vogue to suggest the natural, and cascades, rivers, lakes and streams were thus preferred. At Rousham William Kent introduced a spring head in Venus's Vale and a complicated system of hydraulics, but the vulgarity of a powerful jet or series of jets of water was intolerable. The art of hydraulics was sufficiently understood and the great masterpieces of water manipulation as at Versailles in France and Villa d'Este in Italy were perfectly possible, but the eighteenth-century taste in England preferred the babbling of cascades as at Bowood (Wiltshire), and the more so if they contrived to maintain the water level of the lake at the same time.

'Capability' Brown is known never to have introduced a fountain into any of his schemes, but by the time Repton was designing his flower gardens at the very beginning of the nineteenth century a suggestion of a fountain as a central feature crept in. (The idea of a formal garden with a water spring at its centre was a very ancient one.) At Ashridge (Hertfordshire), for instance, Repton suggested a water conduit at the centre of the little garden he called the Monk's Garden. There is, indeed, a conduit at the centre of the garden of that name at Ashridge, but it is not of the design or location of Repton's plan, though his ideas were certainly upheld.

By the end of the nineteenth century immense fountains were being constructed, some with the elaboration of design that came at that time. The exuberance of water played under pressure was an accepted adjunct to garden design. Paxton's great Emperor Fountain at Chatsworth (Derbyshire) was, and still is, a single jet striking high into the air, but many fountains were accompanied by elaborate statuary, the figures adding to the general play of movement and light. At Waddesdon (Buckinghamshire) the south terrace overlooks a parterre in the Italian style with a large group of Italian statuary enjoying the splashing water. A small but nonetheless dramatic group surrounds a fountain that heralds the entrance to the level forecourt drive of the house.

The cockleshell fountain is in a similar position at Cliveden (Buckinghamshire), white and very pleasing, the focal point at the head of the drive when seen from the house. Bronze exuberance can be found at Ascott, also in Buckinghamshire, where Venus rides in a shell chariot, and best of all at Castle Howard (North Yorkshire), where Hercules holds the world against the spray — a fountain made for the Great Exhibition of 1851.

Smaller and gentler versions, frequently with finer jets of water, add movement to a number of gardens. At Bicton (Devon), for example, in the Italian Gardens there is a tall bowl fountain set in the lawn; at Hever Castle (Kent) there is a gallery of fountains. Other examples are Spetchley Park (Worcestershire), Sezincote (Gloucestershire) — an umbrella-like design, the Amusing jet above the pagoda at Alton Towers (Staffordshire) and a lovely comparative newcomer at Wilton House (Wiltshire) in the forecourt.

Dramatic *jets d'eau* reminiscent of Paxton's creation at Chatsworth are seen no more, but a single jet adds considerable drama to the water campus at the University of York, designed by Frank Clarke, and to the water parterre at Blenheim Palace (Oxfordshire), made in the first decade of the present century. Simple jets in twos and threes are seen at Wisley (Surrey) in the new formal water garden designed by Lanning Roper and Geoffrey Jellicoe, in the water garden at Hemel Hempstead (Hertfordshire) and at Compton Acres (Dorset) in the Italian Garden.

Fountains enjoyed their heyday in Victorian public parks and squares and are now far more restrained in both design and range.

3. Gardens to visit

All the gardens described in the following pages are open regularly. Information about opening times and details of other gardens open to the public are to be found in such publications as: *Historic Houses, Castles and Gardens in Great Britain and Ireland,* an ABC Historic Publication, published annually and usually first on sale in bookshops during January or February; *Gardens of England and Wales Open to the Public,* published annually by the National Gardens Scheme and universally known as 'The Yellow Book', and *Gardens to Visit,* published annually by the Gardener's Sunday Organisation.

Abbotsbury Garden, Abbotsbury, Dorset
This collection of sub-tropical plants started by Countess Ilchester about 1815 is maintained in the form of a woodland garden. No house remains but the garden runs down to the sea. There are many fine old trees, magnolias, camellias and rhododendrons. It is a plantsman's paradise, with a good collection of rare trees and shrubs.

Acorn Bank, Temple Sowerby, near Penrith, Cumbria
A small and somewhat unpromising garden of lawn, roses and shrubs, protected by the National Trust, hides probably the most extensive collection of physic plants in Britain. Within the walled garden a large rectangular plot is sliced by two paths to form borders and a central bed and here many little-grown herbs can be seen. Baneberry, blackroot, madder, skunk cabbage, Indian physic, wild indigo and such economic plants are planted in herbaceous border style with sages, mints, tansy, borage and elecampane.

Alton Towers, near Cheadle, Staffordshire
Part of the grounds is run as an amusement park, but this ought not to deter the serious garden visitor. Started in the nineteenth century by the fifteenth Earl of Shrewsbury, the garden at Alton Towers scales a steep slope and has an almost fanciful quality. Numerous ornaments and buildings are to be discovered among the mature growth: temples, pagodas, cottages, fountains — and horticultural delights also. There are good trees, especially cedars, and much other worthwhile planting, an extensive rock garden and attractive conservatories.

Anglesey Abbey, Lode, near Cambridge
This remarkable garden, created in the twentieth century and now maintained by the National Trust, houses the best collection of statuary out of doors in the British Isles; this was amassed by

24

Lord Fairhaven between 1926 and 1962. The Circular Temple, consisting of ten Corinthian columns surrounded by a clipped hedge and guarded by a pair of stone lions, is one of the most dramatic features of the garden. A copy of Bernini's *David* is the central figure. Much good tree planting, now maturing well, adds interest and the Coronation Avenue of alternate planes and horsechestnuts, planted in 1937, runs absolutely straight for more than half a mile (800m). At right angles there is another avenue and both terminate in a glade or circle of trees.

Antony House, Torpoint, Cornwall

Trees are the dominant feature of this garden and radiating avenues lead away from the house. The tree house like a candle snuffer fashioned in yew is a unique feature and the garden ornament is also unusual. Much of it is Indianesque, the Burmese temple bell being of particular interest.

Arley Hall, near Northwich, Cheshire

Laid out during the nineteenth century, the garden has not been altered in concept. The two great herbaceous borders are thought to be amongst the first established in Britain. They appear on a map of the garden dated 1846. Clipped yew forms deep protective bays and enfolds the whole area of the borders. Note the handsome stone pavilion at the head of the borders. Elsewhere there is a scented garden, some good pleaching, a herb garden and a good collection of old shrub roses. Perhaps the most dramatic feature is the ilex avenue, planted about 1840. The trees (*Quercus ilex*) have been clipped to form tall rotund pillars.

Ascott, Wing, Buckinghamshire

The main impact of the planting at Ascott is the colour. Trees, shrubs, container plants, golden yew hedges, borders and Victorian-style bedding combine to form a very colourful garden in a comparatively small area. It is a little garish for some tastes but a good example of what can be achieved. There are very good trees and an excellent lead fountain representing Venus riding a shell chariot with attendants and fish, all open to the surrounding countryside. A small tufa garden is of interest and beyond the house there is a restrained lily pool with a thatched summerhouse, almost as if the main part of the garden were too much and here is a withdrawing area! Not to be missed to one side of the main lawn is a sundial formed of yew and box, clipped into Roman numerals. Note also two stone dogs near the entrance gates. Ascott is maintained by the National Trust.

Ashridge, near Berkhamsted, Hertfordshire

A level site to the east, south and west of the building at Ashridge is attractively broken up into several smaller gardens and surrounded by Victorian tree planting. The original idea for the smaller gardens came from Humphry Repton in the very early years of the nineteenth century, but his designs were not carried through. A circular rosary, sheltered by a high hedge, and the formal armorial parterre of clipped box in the so-called Monk's Garden probably echo his idea most forcibly. Modern additions include an informal rock garden within a formal setting and a formal sunken rose garden in what was once a skating lake. Rhododendron planting adds interest in early summer and there is a good grotto-like tunnel constructed of flints.

Athelhampton, near Puddletown, Dorset

Begun in the 1890s and added to at intervals since then, the garden at Athelhampton is made up of several smaller self-contained areas carefully interrelated. The basic plan follows that of Inigo Thomas. A modern informal garden is to be found away from the house along the riverbank. The dovecote dominates the lawn near the house and has been renovated. The present owner is carrying out much replanting and renovation to stonework.

Barnsley House, near Cirencester, Gloucestershire

This small garden is full of detail and very good planting; walls, paths, borders and containers are filled with first-class plants. A laburnum arcade and a parterre are formal features, but the almost miniature landscape complete with Gothic summerhouse complements the whole concept. A newly planted vegetable garden planned as a *potager* is of interest and there is a reproduction of a knot garden, very well conceived in trimmed box.

Barrington Court, near Ilminster, Somerset

Several quite separate gardens are linked by doorways to form a most interesting series. Each garden varies, formal and informal, but each is in harmony with its surroundings. Gertrude Jekyll designed some of these gardens and her lavish use of plants, examples of which still remain, in the otherwise formal setting is noteworthy. Sweeping lawns planted to one side of the house with many young trees are a stark contrast to the interest behind the various walls. Near the house is the many-faceted sundial of red stone.

Belsay Hall, Ponteland, Northumberland

Under the guardianship of English Heritage since 1980 this garden has been rescued from neglect and now offers one of the most romantically exciting settings in the north of England. Around the (ruined) hall substantial borders have been replanted and an extensive parterre of Victorian origin recreated which includes domes of *Pieris floribunda.* The winter garden abounds in evergreens and has been extensively planted with heathers. But the glory of Belsay is the walk through the gorge cut into the quarry from which the stone for the hall was obtained. Sheer walls almost exclude the light in parts; ferns and bamboo, ivy and rhododendron in profusion decorate the route — now a grotto, now a glen — which leads to the old castle of Belsay with its neat lawns and spring-time bulbs.

Bicton Gardens, near Budleigh Salterton, Devon

The main area first seen by the visitor is the Italian Garden, backed by a temple, orangeries and a grass terrace which overlook an extensive gently sloping lawn looking towards a formal lake. A fountain plays and large cedars cast their shade. To one side there is a little rock and water garden with a circular pool which houses a collection of shells together with a shell house. But the main attraction at Bicton is the pinetum, a very good collection of trees extending over more than 10 acres (4 ha). Supported by the maritime climate of south Devon, eucalyptuses flourish among hemlocks, planes, palms and many superb conifers. Unique in England is the avenue of Chilean pine *(Araucaria araucana)* — familiarly known as the monkey puzzle — extending 500 yards (450m). The pride of the garden is the Palm House, a splendid example of a very early conservatory.

Biddulph Grange, near Stoke-on-Trent, Staffordshire

This amazing garden owned by the National Trust will be open, probably only to limited numbers at any one time, during the restoration. Unique in its concept and fantasy, it is not everyone's idea of a garden. Ten or more distinct areas are linked by grotto-like tunnels, bridges, winding walks and deep glens, all of which open out into theatrical areas complete with gods, temples and exotic obelisks. Dating from the 1830s, it reflects a crazy collection of scenic representations of countries overseas. Ferns, bamboos, conifers and other evergreens abound, adding to the eeriness and gloom.

Blenheim Palace, Woodstock, Oxfordshire

What the visitor sees today in the garden at Blenheim Palace is mainly the work of 'Capability' Brown in the eighteenth century (including the lake), but the dramatic water parterre was formed in the 1920s. Earlier formal gardens have been removed but a parterre made early in the twentieth century (and not always open) is laid to one side of the Palace, replacing the original formality and setting the right note for the situation. Everything is on a scale suitably stupendous and arresting.

Blickling Hall, near Aylsham, Norfolk

A central level formal garden, punctuated by topiary specimens, is surrounded by a raised terrace walk, where there is some excellent planting. There are interesting plants to be seen also in the dry moat that surrounds the house. Beyond, a little woodland and a temple can be found on raised ground, and to the side of the house there is a surprisingly natural lake and landscape garden. The styles of several periods are brought together to make a seemingly homogeneous whole. The raised terrace around the formal garden is seventeenth-century in concept, the little woodland of the Restoration period type, and the landscape clearly eighteenth-century. The garden is well maintained by the National Trust.

Bodnant, Tal-y-Cafn, Gwynedd

Planted on a lavishly large scale, Bodnant is an excellent garden for a whole day's excursion for the plantsman. Planting began in the newly made garden in about 1900 under the second Baron Aberconway. A series of terraces scales a hillside with wide views of Snowdonia and in the mild climate of the hills many rhododendrons, camellias, arbutus, magnolias and embrothriums flourish together with conifers. The formality of the various levels among the terraces contrasts so well with the lush tree and shrub planting that details such as the canal pool are especially memorable. Bodnant is an excellent example of a garden of the early twentieth century, now to be seen in its full splendour.

Bowood, near Calne, Wiltshire

Bowood is a good example of an eighteenth-century landscape garden, with nineteenth-century terraces near the house. 'Capability' Brown designed the landscape with the lake and the temple on its far bank. The cascade, about 33 feet (10m) high, a seeming tower of mossy rock, is an attractive way of dealing with the outflow of water from the lake. There are many good trees, especially conifers, and the cedars are of particular note.

Bramham Park, near Wetherby, West Yorkshire

Bramham is one of the finest examples of a Restoration-style garden in Britain. Unfortunately a great gale in 1962 destroyed many trees but replanting has taken place, thus affording a unique example of what such gardens looked like in the making. The foresight of their creators and the long-term planting of the late seventeenth and early eighteenth centuries were indeed a dedication to posterity. At Bramham the *allées* (small straight rides through planted woodland) made originally in the first decade of the eighteenth century are now mature in parts and in other areas have been replaced since the early 1960s. The pools, pavilion, urns and other ornaments were originally all part of the great design of the *allées* and the various points of interest to which they lead. The form is taking shape again and it is only by interpreting the living scene that the visitor will derive enjoyment. Near the house there is terracing and a colourful pavement area, suitably planted for seasonal effect.

Branklyn, Perth, Tayside

Now under the care of the National Trust for Scotland, this jewel of a garden was made by a husband and wife, who started in 1922 with very little knowledge. By the mid 1960s a remarkable garden had been made in which almost all available space is given up to plants and the lawn consists merely of grass paths between the various beds. The tapestry of planting is good and the interest to the plantsman infinite; the garden is a fine example of what can be done in a small area. The planting is not over-lavish and yet generous, with good use of ground-cover plants.

Bressingham Hall, near Diss, Norfolk

The lover of hardy herbaceous perennials should not miss the remarkable collection that has been made at Bressingham by Alan Bloom since the 1950s. His use of the island bed, as opposed to the conventional herbaceous border, has been much publicised, but in his garden at Bressingham the design is justified because there has been sufficient space in which to achieve an overall integrated effect. A pool lies at the lowest point of the undulating lawns and the visitor will find innumerable ideas for planting associations. The collection includes many plants rarely cultivated and some little-known cultivars. In recent years Alan Bloom's son has extended the garden with heathers and dwarf conifers.

Brodick Castle, Isle of Arran, Strathclyde

This ancient castle site benefits from the warmth of the Gulf Stream in the west of Scotland and being on the eastern slopes of the Isle of Arran it is sheltered from the fierce Atlantic gales. Under the care of the National Trust for Scotland, the garden is luscious with rhododendrons and tree fern, Australasian plants and many others from the warmer parts of the world. Apart from a sheltered enclosed old kitchen garden now planted with ornamental plants the site is a woodland one with rocks and water. Most of the planting has been done since 1930 and it is a well maintained collection of considerable interest.

Broughton Hall, near Skipton, North Yorkshire

The approach to Broughton Hall is across parkland but the visitor will be surprised to find the most intriguing Victorian fantasy beside and behind the house. To the east is a probably unique *tapis vert* on a sloping site formed in clipped box. It was designed by W. A. Nesfield. An intricate design of scrolls is formed in box, and spar and gravel are scattered as a background. Grass scrolls repeat the idea in a broader pattern to form the border to the whole formal garden. A surrounding boundary is punctuated by a small pavilion. Behind the house the land rises very steeply but a Victorian conservatory, also designed by Nesfield, stretches out from the house and has a domed chamber. Here is an example of unspoilt Victoriana at its best, free from the clutter of adornment.

Burford House (Salop), near Tenbury Wells, Worcestershire

Here a modern garden of plants has been made since 1950 around an early eighteenth-century house of brick. Formal terracing and pools give way to the highlight of the garden, a variety of irregular beds, with a stream and boggy areas and smooth lawn. An overall feeling of space has been achieved, making good use of the surroundings and of the plants themselves. Hardy perennials and foliage plants have been well used and many plant associations are extremely pleasing. The visitor will learn much and leave with many ideas which may be adapted to far smaller gardens.

Buscot Park, near Faringdon, Oxfordshire

The garden, really a formal glade, was created at the very beginning of the twentieth century in the Italian style by Harold Peto, a garden designer. It connects the house with the lake and consists of little more than a small canal or stream which flows the length of the *allée,* sometimes as a moving water and sometimes, cleverly, as almost still and reflective water. Ornaments and statuary decorate the walk and a formal pool with a pleasing stone fountain heads the vista. This is a garden to be enjoyed by the aesthetically inclined visitor.

Castle Ashby, near Northampton, Northamptonshire

Away to the east the Brown landscape can still be enjoyed and a walk curves around the lake and past a temple. In the mid nineteenth century a large terrace was made at the eastern side of the house, the work reputed to have been either designed or suggested by Sir Charles Barry. The parterre remains, planted with colourful modern planting, and the stone balustrade surrounding it encloses a biblical quotation in stone.

Away from the formal garden to the south-east is a well matured garden in the Italian style with quite good shrub planting and some interesting roses and clematis on the walls. Here are one or two old greenhouses, and a remarkable stone camellia-type glasshouse, designed by Sir Digby Wyatt with a curious stone spiral staircase to the upper floor.

Henry Compton, Bishop of London in the late seventeenth century, was a member of the family which owns this estate, and he was one of the first patrons of plant hunters and plant introductions.

The estate avenues were planted in 1695.

Castle Howard, near Malton, North Yorkshire

The early design for the garden at Castle Howard was begun at the start of the eighteenth century and set out to be a formal garden on a grand scale to accompany the mansion that the architect, Vanbrugh, was designing. As the years passed and taste progressed towards the more natural landscape garden, the splendid site on the Yorkshire hillside at Castle Howard was transformed into the most splendid of all landscape gardens. Today the formal areas around the house are on a large scale, with seasonal planting and a dramatic fountain at the central point. Curving away from the house and traversing the hillside is a broad grass terrace which leads to an enormous panoramic landscape and, finally, to the Temple of the Four Winds. Below there is a lake with walks which lead back to the formal garden behind the house. Beyond is a bridge and mausoleum, all so much a part of the landscape that it is hard to believe that they have been planned. A remarkable collection of old shrub roses has been assembled during the past few years.

Charlecote Park, near Stratford-upon-Avon, Warwickshire

The driveway approaches the pink brick Jacobean-style house, of Victorian date, through a brick Tudor gatehouse. The gatehouse is very attractive and was built in 1588; the upper rooms are now a museum of the Lucy family. The area between the gatehouse and the house is now grassed over and was the Elizabethan courtyard. The walls that bound it have attractive ornamental balustrading. Beyond the house simple terracing and steps lead down to the river Avon, and beyond can be seen the deer park and some work of 'Capability' Brown. (The visitor should not miss a painting which hangs in the drawing room of the house, depicting the formal Dutch garden which surrounded the house in the seventeenth century and was cleared away by Brown.)

To one side of the house there is a small attractive garden where the National Trust has made a collection of herbs mentioned by Shakespeare and there is shrub planting elsewhere in this part of the garden. An orangery flanks one side of the lawn. A few pretty statues, in eighteenth-century style and moulded in lead, stand at the entrance to this side garden.

Chartwell, Westerham, Kent

Chartwell was the home of Sir Winston Churchill and some of the details of the garden appear in his paintings—the black swans, for example, which inhabit the twin lakes at the foot of the valley. The house itself stands at the top of a small escarpment. The garden falls away below and to the north the slope is scaled by a series of little pools and waterfalls, all lost in planting. A stout pergola leads to a pavilion, aptly named the Marlborough Pavilion. At the opposite side of the house is the former kitchen garden, now used as an ornamental flower garden and approached by a path flanked by yellow roses, planted to commemorate the golden wedding of Sir Winston and Lady Churchill. Pretty contrasting grey-leaved plants like senecio and nepeta are planted beneath the roses. In this area of the garden there is also a flight of steps flanked by lavender and a marvellous view over the Weald can be seen.

Chatsworth, near Bakewell, Derbyshire

Chatsworth is a garden primarily architectural in design and dramatic in concept as it scales a hillside in the Peak District. But there is also splendid planting to be seen. A rose garden, well stocked with all sorts of roses, flourishes in spite of the chalk soil, and there are many perennials of interest too. An area of hillside behind the house forms a wild garden with woodland walks and there is also a valuable pinetum begun about 1830. In early summer the Azalea Dell and rock garden provide attraction. But it is the water garden and the glass for which Chatsworth is famous. The seventeenth-century work of London and Wise, the great sparkling water staircase called the Cascade, still falls down the hillside. It emerges from several sources through the Cascade House at the head of the slope and runs to the large Canal Pool, in which the house is reflected. Sir Joseph Paxton added the single-jet Emperor Fountain. He is best remembered as the architect of the Crystal Palace in London. The prototype for this was his great conservatory at Chatsworth, which was demolished soon after the First World War. It has been replaced by a new house of modern design supported externally by gantries and cables. An attractive range of camellia houses remains at Chatsworth, reminiscent of estate gardening in Victorian times.

Chenies Manor House (Bucks), near Rickmansworth, Hertfordshire

There is evidence of a garden around this Tudor manor house for centuries and since the mid 1960s it has been restored, redesigned and planted in a most lavish and attractive way. Lawns and mature trees around the house give way to a rectangular sunken garden based on the original one at Hampton Court. Here the planting is of perennials and interspersed with summer plants and spring bulbs, and dotted with standard roses, a true summer garden. To one side is an enclosed white garden abounding with white-flowered plants and silver foliage and furnished with clipped, solid forms of box and yew to provide an arresting contrast to the profusion of the summer

1. *The Burmese bell in the gardens of Antony House in Cornwall.*
2. *The balustraded terrace in the formal gardens at Athelhampton in Dorset.*

3. The palm house at Bicton Gardens, south Devon, was originally
an eighteenth-century orangery.

4. At Blenheim Palace, Oxfordshire, the immense water parterre is
dramatic in impact.

5. Overlooking the nineteenth-century parterre to the Thames beyond, at Cliveden, in Buckinghamshire.
6. The Emperor Fountain at Chatsworth, Derbyshire.

7. *The mausoleum at Castle Howard, North Yorkshire.*

8. Built in 1960 as a memorial to Dorothy Elmhirst, this summer-house is in the grounds of Dartington Hall, Devon.

9. The armorial parterre at Edzell Castle, Tayside, in Scotland, is surrounded by an elaborately decorated wall.

10. The replanted box parterre on the south side of Elvaston Castle, Derbyshire.
11. One of the fine walks and herbaceous borders at Forde Abbey in Dorset.

12. *A lily pond in the garden designed by Gertrude Jekyll at Hestercombe in Somerset.*

13. A mixed border at Hidcote Manor in Gloucestershire.

14. *Formal Victorian gardens by the house at Holker Hall, Cumbria.*
15. *The topiary specimens at Levens Hall, Cumbria, laid out in 1692.*

16. The formal eighteenth-century terraced garden at Mapperton, Dorset, is set within the surrounding, natural countryside.
17. At Montacute, Somerset, the simplicity of the formal garden contrasts with the elaborate Elizabethan walls and richly planted courtyard garden behind them.

18. Robert Bakewell's wrought-iron arbour is an eyecatcher in the garden at Melbourne Hall, Derbyshire.

19. At Packwood House, Warwickshire, bee boles made to receive lipwork beehives are built into the seventeenth-century wall.
20. The hanging garden at Powis Castle, Powys, Wales.

21. *The Chinese bridge at Pusey House, Oxfordshire.*
22. *The hornbeam arbour at St Fagan's Castle, South Glamorgan.*

23. *The rock garden and fern collection at Sizergh Castle, Cumbria, is dominated by the castle chimneys.*

24. The view to the Pantheon across the lake at Stourhead, Wiltshire, in early spring.
25. The Great Conservatory at Syon Park, near London, was built by Charles Fowler in the 1820s.

26. A view across one of the formal canals at Westbury Court, Gloucestershire.
27. The Palladian bridge that spans the river Nadder at Wilton House, Wiltshire, is one of three such bridges in England.

garden. A bowling alley (on the site of an ancient one) and borders full of sweetly scented plants make this ə garden of delightful surprises, yet reminiscent of a Tudor court garden. The remarkable physic garden, laid out in 1976, is now mature. Beds are allocated to medicinal plants, dye plants, culinary and legendary plants. This a gardener's garden.

Clapton Court, near Crewkerne, Dorset

The marriage of formal terracing, formal water garden and levels with an informal rock garden and shrub planting at Clapton Court is masterly. Beyond the main garden a hillside has been planted up in recent years to form a woodland garden with a stream, where numerous botanically interesting plants are to be seen. A feature of the whole garden is that all the plants are labelled, so making a visit a delight to the plant enthusiast. Several garden areas lead on one from another without being closely departmented as in so many other gardens. A good rose garden at the back of the house, borders of hardy perennials and good climbing plants are all well tended. But one of the best features is the woodland and ground cover planting along the main drive. There is a specialist garden centre for fuchsias.

Claremont Landscape, Esher, Surrey

The woodland adjacent to the house at Claremont is being renovated by the National Trust. The house is now a girl's school and is apart from the landscape garden. The area is one of the earliest surviving landscape gardens, probably made in the very early years of the eighteenth century. There is a lake, temple, grotto, belvedere and a large amphitheatre, constructed in turf, which is being cleared. Vistas and views from various vantage points make a visit well worthwhile.

Claverton Manor, near Bath, Avon

The house at Claverton is the home of the American Museum in Britain but the garden is quite recently planted, except for many of the trees. Borders around the house and below the terrace are rich in shrubs and herbaceous perennials. Many unusual plants such as angelica are used decoratively. There is also a very small representative herb garden with an old straw bee skep as its focal point and a small collection of dye plants. But on a lower level the chief delight is a formal rose and flower garden, a reproduction of that made at Mount Vernon, Virginia, by George Washington. The beds are surrounded by clipped box and the paths are trim with raked gravel. A neat white fence surrounds it.

Cliveden (Buckinghamshire), near Maidenhead, Berkshire

There is much of interest at Cliveden for the garden visitor and it is very well maintained by the National Trust. The approach

drive is through tree and shrub planting, much of it rhododendron, until a gleaming white cockleshell fountain is reached and
the broad approach to the house is seen. Wide lawns are flanked
first by woodland and later by good herbaceous borders, and there
are a few very old mulberry trees as well. Beyond the house lies the
glory of Cliveden, the great parterre. A simple but enormous
pattern of beds with clipped box spreads over the lawn in a great
arc, and the woodland and river Thames beyond form part of the
same man-made scene but appear to be completely natural.
Various walks through the woods return to the cockleshell
fountain, passing through several interesting gardens. There is an
open air theatre, a pavilion and, most rewarding of all, the Long
Garden with its great scrolls of clipped box and statues. On the
walls in this garden is an interesting collection of plants, *Dipelta
floribunda, Azara microphylla, Calycanthus* species, *Staphylia
colchica,* with roses and clematis. Crossing over the main drive
once more, the path leads to a Japanese garden made by the late
Lord Astor, fashioned around a kidney-shaped lake and com-
pleted with a highly coloured pagoda made first for the Great
Exhibition in 1851, surmounted by a 'rampant little dragon'.

Corsham Court, near Chippenham, Wiltshire

Good trees are the salient feature of the garden at Corsham
Court. A beautiful walnut, London plane (widely layered) and a
Ginkgo biloba are specially noteworthy. But the visitor with an
enquiring mind will enjoy the landscape created by 'Capability'
Brown and 'improved' by Repton in the eighteenth century and see
the bath house designed by John Nash — a seemingly Gothic
pavilion with crocketed pinnacles. Beyond this there is an ornamental flower garden with some attractive shrub planting and a
curious serpentine wall made to represent a ruin.

Cotehele House, near Calstock, Cornwall

The grey granite house atop a steeply wooded garden forms a
memorable setting, especially in early spring when the camellias,
magnolias and azaleas are in flower. The National Trust is
responsible for the upkeep and to wander down the steep slope
beside the natural stream and waterfalls to the pool below is a
gardener's delight. The scene is enhanced by a lovely beehive-
shaped granite dovecote set to one side of the glen. Near the house
simple terracing and lawns are kept trim and on the other side at
the approach to the house narcissi are naturalised in the grass, so
that a spring visit is a delight.

Cranborne Manor, Cranborne, Dorset

A wide range of interesting plants is to be found at Cranborne
Manor, including many with old-fashioned associations or herbal

qualities, and all have been introduced with keen discernment. The entrance courtyard of pink brick is planted with restrained colour — soft pinks, beige and grey — and a wide variety of wall plants flourishes there. To one side is an old-world knot garden and beyond there is a mount, known to John Tradescant and now surrounded by beds of shrub roses and lavenders. Further on, through the white garden, a path has been made along the river and includes a small chequerboard area planted with a collection of thymes. At the other side of the house an avenue of pleached limes skirts a rectangular lawn, and a pergola the second side. Beyond is the old kitchen garden with a double border of cottage plants, a delight to the visitor at all seasons. Bedding plants, bulbs, annuals, hardy perennials, apple trees and roses all grow together and the beds are usually edged with daisies or pansies. The most remarkable feature of the garden at Cranborne Manor is the herb garden set apart across the main drive and screened by a high cob wall and yew hedge. Formal in concept, it is one of the best herb gardens of the present day and contains a great many plants not often seen in such collections.

Crathes Castle, near Banchory, Grampian

The garden at Crathes Castle consists of a series of gardens or rooms, each planted differently but all surprisingly well integrated. This treatment increases the amount of shelter and enables many worthwhile plants to be grown. Near the house there are several small formal gardens, one with a pool encircled by clipped yews and pleasant planting in bronzes and gold. A blue garden and an enormous herbaceous border cunningly maintained in planting of the same colour are criss-crossed by white borders. There is also a yellow and gold garden. Below the house the land falls away steeply and is well terraced so that there are congenial homes for a large variety of shrubs against the walls: *Hoheria* species, Euchryphias and the lemon-flowered *Illicium anisatum*. The National Trust for Scotland administers the garden and maintains the glasshouses with an interesting selection of tender plants.

Dalemain, near Penrith, Cumbria

The ancient estate at Dalemain certainly dates from Saxon times and the pele tower of the present house is Norman. On the north side of the house the garden occupies the site of a medieval settlement and it is interesting to see that at one side of this courtyard a raised bed has been made recently and is being planted. Beyond, a little formal water garden is a feature not to be missed. It is probably the remains of a former knot garden, probably Elizabethan, and the little pool and fountain have been added as a central point of interest. A Victorian greenhouse is to the east, and beyond the land rises across a glorious mêlée of orchard and flower garden, so natural in concept that it might have 'just happened'. At one side of this area is an Elizabethan summerhouse or gazebo, from which to overlook the surrounding park and meadows to the west. Along the western terrace of the house a high wall backs a border of mixed planting and in front of the house is eighteenth-century parkland.

Dartington Hall, near Totnes, Devon

Although there is evidence of an older site at Dartington and some very old trees, the present garden has been made during the past thirty-five years. The old tilt yard has been turned into an ideal open-air theatre with a surrounding terrace of turved steps for spectators. To one side the site commands a superb view over the countryside beyond, and behind there is a row of well trimmed Irish yews.

The woodland garden, where azaleas, rhododendrons, camellias and magnolias bloom in early summer, is reached by a dramatic flight of steps. The visitor might be forgiven for not mounting the stairs, but the change in style to woodland is so well contrived that it would be a pity to miss it.

Drummond Castle, near Crieff, Tayside

The great parterre at Drummond Castle is the most remarkable in the British Isles not only for its immensity but also for the intricacy of the design. It was made in the nineteenth century on a site where there had been a similar garden for two hundred years and covers 13 acres (5 ha). The visitor comes upon it quite suddenly after passing through a courtyard and both the scale and the design are astonishing. Statues, topiary, carpet bedding and trim lawns combine to decorate this confection of garden art. Beyond it the eye is carried along a wide vista through woodland over a rising slope, emphasising the pattern below.

Dyffryn, St Nicholas, Cardiff, South Glamorgan

The garden at Dyffryn is a memorial to Reginald Cory, an important horticultural personality of the early twentieth century. He commissioned Thomas Mawson, a leading landscape architect, to design the garden and then set about making a remarkable collection of plants, many of them dating from the original introductions. The basic design remains recognisable and the great lawns studded with formal beds, the long herbaceous borders, rose garden and plant houses provide a delight of colour all the year round. In contrast there is the arboretum with many remarkable trees, shrubs and informal corners. The terrace in front of the house overlooks the formal water garden, and to right and left secret enclosed gardens offer delights to attract most inclinations.

Edzell Castle, Edzell, Tayside

Here is a rectangular garden completely enclosed in the manner of a medieval garden. The site has been used as a garden since 1604, though there were some years of neglect during the nineteenth century.

The formality is stark, with carpet bedding and clipped box almost too prim for the design. The pattern was restored only in the 1930s but the garden is not to be missed. It is surrounded by a decorative wall, in which chequerboard panels of niches are scooped, designed to accommodate boxes of flowering plants. Various other niches were possibly intended for busts or urns. Holes allow birds to nest within the cavity of the wall and decorative panels depict the arts and deities. At one corner of the garden is a garden house, questionably a gazebo, in the same rose sandstone as the wall and the castle itself.

Elvaston Castle, near Derby, Derbyshire

Set amid somewhat unpromising woodland with criss-crossing drives, the garden immediately surrounding the building is rewarding. An immense box parterre is spread in front of the building, of both the green and golden forms of box, and beyond it is a unique lychgate fashioned in yew. The roof of this gate is of considerable age and appears in illustrations made at the end of the nineteenth century. To one side of the parterre is the old 'elephant' hedge of yew and large specimens of topiary are dotted over a rectangular garden. Leading away from this, woodland paths are bordered by fairly general planting. But set apart from the main area is the old walled kitchen garden, within which there is a wealth of interest. Herbaceous plants like hostas and several unusual shrubs, notably *Physocarpus opulifolia*, are planted in bold beds and the walls support tender climbers like *Mutisia ilicifolia* and protect choice specimens such as *Myrtus apiculata*.

Forde Abbey (Dorset), near Chard, Somerset

The dominant feature of the garden at Forde Abbey is the Long Pond, a canal of unruffled water which reflects the front of the massive building. Beyond is a mount and to one side a woodland bog garden, very well planted with primulas, trilliums, astilbes, irises and other bog-loving plants. Water plays a great part in the garden and this boggy area leads to the Mermaid Pond planted with waterlilies. Across the pond is a rectangular tree house made of beech, behind which the garden opens out to rising lawns. Here is a garden made within an eighteenth-century landscape and the ha-ha boundary is a good example.

Walking back towards the house there are good mature conifers, pleasant shrubs, herbaceous planting and a rock garden. A white wisteria forms a canopy over the entrance porch to the house, and inside is a winter garden which runs the length of the building, often remarkably decorative with plants grown in pots. Behind the building is a kitchen garden now used as a nursery, garden centre and practical fruit garden.

Glendurgan, near Falmouth, Cornwall

A particularly fine collection of flowering trees is to be found at Glendurgan, made during the second half of the nineteenth century. Benefiting from the mild climate of south-west England, the rare and beautiful trees are seen at their best. In spring magnolias, camellias, rhododendrons and euchryphias abound in this woodland garden with underplanting of shrubs and bulbous plants. Across a sloping hillside is a remarkable maze, unusually fashioned in laurel, and not symmetrical like the accepted labyrinth.

Gravetye Manor, near East Grinstead, West Sussex

Of particular interest to the garden historian, Gravetye Manor was the home of William Robinson, the plantsman whose influence upon natural-style garden design has been so powerful. Here he created a woodland garden, now more familiarly called a wild garden, early in the twentieth century. Around the house, which is now a country hotel, the formal terracing is softened by permanent planting of shrubs, sub-shrubs and woody perennials. The garden has been neglected in the intervening years and is not exactly as Robinson left it, but it has been well renovated and faithfully represents his own garden.

Great Dixter, Northiam, East Sussex

An interesting collection of hardy perennials is to be seen at Great Dixter, a garden maintained by the Lloyd family, who have contributed much to the culture of these plants. The house was enlarged by the architect Edwin Lutyens early in the twentieth century and the influence of Gertrude Jekyll on the planting is apparent although she did not work at Great Dixter herself. This and the keen interest of the present owner, Christopher Lloyd, in hardy perennials ensures that there are many interesting plants for the garden visitor to see. The plants are used to good overall effect, especially in the area to the side of the house and along the terraces, where sympathetic planting shows what can be achieved by careful use of complementary plant material. Elsewhere there is a lawn and a display of topiary and many shrubs and climbers. A rose garden is a separate feature and there is an enclosed courtyard as well as a small formal garden with an octagonal pool at its centre. As in many twentieth-century gardens, separate cells or rooms have been created which add surprise as one progresses round the garden.

Haddon Hall, near Bakewell, Derbyshire

For rose lovers the garden at Haddon Hall in summer is a delight. Numerous other shrubs and perennial plants are there as well, but the informal use of roses against the old stone terracing and walls is very attractive. The house of Haddon Hall is perched atop an escarpment and the garden consists of a series of steep terraces happily linked by good stone staircases and embellished with old balustrading.

Hampton Court, Greater London

Cardinal Wolsey started the garden at Hampton Court in 1514 when he was building his magnificent palace. Since then the garden has undergone many changes with the varying tastes and inclinations of each period. The most dramatic of the changes were made during the reign of William and Mary, when London and Wise, famous nurserymen and garden designers, redesigned much of the garden. They were responsible for the radiating avenues and the canal pool which can be seen today. Everything is on an immense scale, dwarfing the statuary and screens, all in a style known in England before the advent of the eighteenth-century landscape garden. The formal gardens on the southern side of the palace, though known as the Tudor gardens, were planned in the eighteenth century. The so-called knot garden was made in the twentieth century. Another modern innovation is the rose garden in the former tilt yard. The maze, a familiar garden pastime in Wolsey's time, is a more recent version than his labyrinth, and elsewhere the shrubs and ornamental flower gardens are a twentieth-century representation.

Hardwick Hall, near Chesterfield, Derbyshire

Hardwick Hall is a great Elizabethan mansion built by Bess of Hardwick. The garden seen today has all been made since late Victorian times but its simplicity is appealing. An enclosed garden by the house is planted with shrubs and climbing plants and the walls to the south of the building back a good perennial border of mixed planting. Beyond this the basic plan is cruciform: an alley of yew runs north to south and crosses one formed in hornbeam running east to west, thus forming four roughly shaped rectangles. Two of these are orchard, one of which is devoted to the planting of nut trees — a practice of former days — and a third rectangle is a rose garden. But the fourth contains a large collection of herbs and old economic plants. The National Trust has made this collection since the mid 1960s and recently it has been replanned and extended. In it there are huge wigwams of wood entwined with hops and along one side there is a hedge of *Rosa rubiginosa*.

Harlow Car, Harrogate, North Yorkshire

The garden of the Northern Horticultural Society at Harrogate has been made completely since the Second World War and is a remarkable achievement. It demonstrates what can be done in an elevated position in a harsh climate. Use has been made in the design of a natural stream that runs at the foot of a valley towards the old spa town, and the length of the stream is splendidly planted with primulas, astilbes and other bog-loving plants. Trees and shrubs and great clumps of woody perennials give the planting a luscious air hardly to be expected in that location. A rose garden and several demonstration plots, woodland areas and two good rock gardens and scree beds are to be found. Not to be missed is a lovely area planted with shrub roses.

Hatfield House, Hatfield, Hertfordshire

The immensity of scale at Hatfield is matched only by the wide range of plants. Below the terraces the Jacobean garden is laid out in a series of box-edged beds, profuse with mixed planting of shrubs and perennials, and the surrounding elaborate walls support numerous interesting climbing plants. Behind the house is a remarkable garden abounding in flowering perennials set in island beds, with a fountain at the centre. To one side, beyond an old pleached lime walk, is a huge knot garden, the newest addition to this ancient garden and set in front of the old Bishop's Palace. The beds are traced in box edging and are planted with countless simple plants known in Tudor days. Beyond is an extensive fragrant garden with old shrub roses, treasured old wallflowers and garden pinks, honeysuckles and every imaginable aromatic herb.

Heale House, Woodford, near Salisbury, Wiltshire

The garden was laid out at the end of the nineteenth century in the style of the period and today represents the epitome of an English garden. Borders and sweeping lawns with some good mature trees offer innumerable delights to the visitor. Many lovely cottage garden plants, old shrub roses and sweet smelling flowers are grown informally in borders and in the old kitchen garden with its mellowed walls. The river Avon enfolds the site and an attractive Japanese and water garden is set beside it. An authentic Japanese tea house and whimsical dragon-red bridge stand among acers and magnolias — lovely in spring.

Hergest Croft, Kington, Herefordshire

The garden at Hergest Croft is famous for its trees and shrubs and the area around the house is a good lesson in permanent planting. The garden is divided into two parts: the rolling lawn and shrub planting near the house, and a pretty wooded area on a lower level away from the building and known as Park Wood. A fine collection of rhododendrons and azaleas is assembled here and everywhere there are good and unusual trees and shrubs collected since the nineteenth century from all parts of the temperate world.

Hestercombe, Kingston St Mary, near Taunton, Somerset

The garden at Hestercombe was designed by Gertrude Jekyll and Edwin Lutyens. About 1960, when in a neglected condition, it became the headquarters of the Somerset Fire Brigade. During the 1960s the firemen tended the garden, doing their best to retain old planting and to clear the straight narrow channels of water and small pools that were a characteristic of the garden. Miss Jekyll's original planting plan was discovered in a shed at Hestercombe and happily funds have been forthcoming for the restoration of the garden to its former splendour.

The garden consists of a large level parterre surrounded by raised walks and on the far-side there is a stone pillared pergola. Several levels are broken by steps and elaborately decorated doorways and arched recesses. To the east there is another garden of formal shape where the levels and stonework continue around the orangery although the planting is informal, and beyond and on a different level is a formal rose garden where the design of the beds is repeated in the woodwork of the gate. Beyond this and behind the house is a derelict cascade and landscape area in a wooded glen.

Hidcote Manor, near Chipping Campden, Gloucestershire

Perhaps the supreme example of a garden based upon a series of garden rooms, the plan of Hidcote garden defies description. It is a long narrow series arranged in a chain-like sequence and linked by narrow paths. At the lowest part there is a stream probably completely natural — or so it would appear, but a step to the other side of the hedge and one is in a stark formal garden planted in lime greens. The visitor will find hedges, topiary, good colour planting, interesting woodland treatment and trees and shrubs. Hidcote is not to everybody's taste, but there are good plants to capture the interest and many new ideas. Noteworthy are the theatre lawn suggesting space in the otherwise complicated garden and the walk leading to attractive wrought iron gates, whence there is a view over the Cotswolds.

Hodnet Hall, near Market Drayton, Salop

In spring and early summer colour and bloom abound in this garden. The area around the house is formal and quite simple but the riot of colour is in the woodland and water garden below. From the terrace of the house perched on a plateau a view above the woodland suggests a former eighteenth-century landscape garden, but as the staircase descends, flanked by heathers, the visitor enters a wonderful garden of colour and sweet scents. Flowering cherries, magnolias, rhododendrons and woodland planting form the canopy for primulas, musks, forget-me-nots, astilbes and ferns that abound in great patches along the length of the water garden. The garden has been made since about 1930 and all the planting is modern.

Holdenby House, Northampton

The main part of the garden which originally surrounded this former Elizabethan palace is under meadow grass, but the terraces and ponds are clearly discernible. The present garden has been restored as a replica in miniature of the original garden and is planted with shrubs and plants that would have been known in the late sixteenth century. A scented garden called the Tootoo Fragrant Border is named after a Victorian dog buried there! The old walled kitchen garden is being restored, probably as a herb garden, but certainly in some way appropriate to its former use. The two huge arches inscribed '1583' given an indication of the scale of the original building and courtyard.

Holker Hall, Cark-in-Cartmel, Cumbria

The greater part of the parkland and garden seen today at Holker Hall is Victorian. There is a good selection of trees in the woodland areas: sorbus, stewartia, cornus, camellia, magnolia and rhododendrons. But it is in the spacious formal area of the garden that the interest lies for the general garden visitor. On a level site set behind the house there are formal rose beds interplanted with agapanthus and then with echiums for ground cover, but beyond on the site of an orangery is an Edwardian rose garden. It was designed by Thomas Mawson. The garden is semicircular in form, bordered by a low balustrade and lavender hedge, and it is backed by a wall which supports some good planting.

Inverewe, Poolewe, near Gairloch, Highland

This garden in north-western Scotland benefits from its mild climate and in late spring the craggy setting comes to life with a flourish. It is set on a peninsula jutting out into a sea loch, and so thin was the original soil that more had to be imported before planting could begin. It is mainly a woodland garden, with trees providing shelter for more tender plants, and there is a complex of winding paths and stone steps. There are also rock walls and a rock bed below, peat beds, a herbaceous border, a pond and an area known amusingly as Bambooselem, where bamboos and tender plants flourish together with flowering trees and climbers. It is mainly for its rich variety of plants that Inverewe is visited, especially for its meconopsis and primulas, even more than for the mountain scenery.

Kiftsgate Court, near Chipping Campden, Gloucestershire

The approach to Kiftsgate Court is along the side of a lawn backed by a wall on which espalier pears are grown, but to the side of and behind the house there is a garden rich in colour combinations and luxuriant growth, perhaps at its best in high summer when the roses are in bloom.

There are rectangular gardens on two sides of the house, one with a fountain and a pool and restrained planting in silver and white — tree peonies, roses, santolinas and flowering bulbs like alliums and erythroniums in the early part of the summer. The other rectangular garden is a formal treatment of four box-edged beds of peonies and shrubs. But joining these two plots, and running alongside them, is a splendid double mixed border, where there are many superbly colourful plants to be seen on either side of a wide central grass path. Below, and curving back below the house, is a series of paths and levels which traverse a steep slope and culminate in a dramatic flight of steps leading to a lower lawn and bathing pool. But, looking back from there, the house appears to perch atop a cliff, which itself is richly planted, combining rocky areas with good retaining walls and a large summerhouse, surrounded by many trees and shrubs.

Knightshayes Court, near Tiverton, Devon

Apart from mature hedges and trees the garden at Knightshayes Court has been made since about 1950 and in the 1970s the National Trust has joined the Knightshayes Trust in administration. Perhaps the wooded area is the most interesting, because lovely trees are underplanted with informal island beds where imaginative planting has been carried out and a wide and rich variety of plants that flourish in open woodland provides almost continuous interest. In the more formal parts, there is a single circular garden surrounded by a yew hedge, decorated by a simple white statue that looks down to a circular pool. The sunken garden, though simple in form, is decoratively planted in mauves and pinks with silver-leaved plants and at one side some joke topiary depicts a fox and hounds scampering silently along the top of a clipped yew hedge.

Lanhydrock, near Bodmin, Cornwall

The formal garden at Lanhydrock is built within the low boundary wall that links the house, church and gatehouse. Clipped yews stand at intervals around it echoing the shape of the decorative finials of the walls and of the gatehouse. The scene is one of architectural precision. Behind the house the hillside is richly planted with beautiful and interesting trees, many of them exotics, which flourish in the favourable climate.

Leonardslee, near Horsham, West Sussex

This garden has been cared for by the Loder family since Victorian times and many fine rhododendrons have been raised here. The best known is *Rhododendron loderi*. The garden is a hillside criss-crossed by paths at various levels and planted with oak, ilex, magnolias, cornus, flowering cherries, camellias, palms and many unusual conifers. Rhododendrons and azaleas abound and in spring and again in autumn the whole hillside is a canopy of colour, sloping down to a warm valley watered by a series of hammer ponds. (Occasionally open is another garden nearby, also planted by the Loder family, at High Beeches. It is particularly beautiful in spring and autumn for the effect of similar plants, but here they are arranged in a dell that one has to discover across a somewhat unpromising landscape.)

Levens Hall, near Kendal, Cumbria

The most memorable feature of the garden at Levens Hall is the topiary specimens which tower in fantastic geometric forms. They have been fashioned of both green and golden yew and of box; although not all are ancient, many were undoubtedly planted in the seventeenth century. The topiary garden with its high hedges is a good example of the decoration the Stuarts added to their gardens. To one side there is a delightful rose garden and to the other several good mixed borders with old orchard trees scattered behind. Some of the trees support splendid climbing plants like clematis and roses. Large clipped beech hedges shelter this part of the garden, forming a kind of *rond point* of grass paths.

Not to be missed is the park at Levens, where, beyond the garden, the main east-west avenue continues out into the countryside. There is a woodland walk to be followed to the valley of the river Kent, where tree planting appears to have been carried out in the making of a landscape garden at the turn of the eighteenth century. The avenue of oaks, a mile (1.6 km) in length, is centred on the river gorge so that the visitor who takes the time to walk to the landscape garden will not be disappointed.

Mapperton, Beaminster, Dorset

The first glimpse of the garden proper at Mapperton is an arresting scene. One looks down upon a large rectangular garden, constructed on various levels, the lowest part at its centre. This long narrow valley was turned into a garden in the 1930s but has all the timelessness of its eighteenth-century character, complete with orangery. Beyond, the former fish tanks have been incorporated into a decorative water garden scheme and the steep banks of the valley well planted with a good range of interesting shrubs. The gully extends out into the surrounding countryside landscape, with a further very good collection of trees and shrubs. At the farthest point an

Embothrium coccineum, the Chilean fire bush, makes a striking feature at the head of the bogside walk in early June.

Melbourne Hall, Melbourne, Derbyshire

The garden at Melbourne is in two main sections and, while it is of special interest to the garden historian, the theme is somewhat obscure. This garden remains as an example of garden design of the first decade of the eighteenth century, when splendid French-style *allées* and formal water were fashionable. But it has not been well maintained over the years, so the plan has become blurred and changed. The visitor will, however, enjoy the wide sweeping lawns in front of the house bordered by big hedges and rolling down to a large lily pool. Great Basin, beyond which is a delightful wrought iron arbour (see page 11). Behind this and slightly to the south is a complex of rides and *allées* with fountains and ornaments at the intersections. This woodland or *bosquet* area covers 10 acres (4 ha). At the highest point, where several *allées* meet, there is a beautiful lead vase by Van Nost, the Vase of the Four Seasons. The main alley runs down from here past a formal pool and fountain back to the iron arbour. Other examples of Van Nost's statuary are at each side of the main parterre, set in bays of yew, where a series of related *Quarrelling Boys* are to be seen. Note also two blackamoors on the upper lawn supporting sundials, and hard by the flower beds are plant containers decorated with handles to resemble Victorian flower baskets.

Montacute, near Yeovil, Somerset

Always quoted as an 'Elizabethan garden', Montacute is an excellent example of an Elizabethan house and walls with finials and gazebos of the period, but the garden itself is modern. The original courtyard has become the enclosed garden with lawns and flower beds below the walls. These borders are tastefully planted with climbers, roses and flowering perennials and were designed by Vita Sackville-West for the National Trust. The lower lawn, to the side of the house, is simply treated with a formal balustraded lily pool and clipped yews, and at the head of the terrace which runs alongside there is an orangery which is now kept furnished with decorative plants. The present drives were not part of the original plan but the woodland planting and the high yew hedges shelter the whole garden and make it very pleasant.

Mottisfont Abbey, near Romsey, Hampshire

At Mottisfont a wide level lawn spreads around the house, built on the site of a former abbey. Large and beautiful trees are dotted about. At one side the river Test winds along and a riverside walk leads to a little garden building. A terrace at the front of the house overlooks a rather unexpected small parterre or knot garden tucked well in towards the building. Beyond there are good blue

Atlas cedars, sweet chestnuts, ilex, copper beeches, planes and other trees and, tracing the direction of the drive, a small fence of pleached limes. But the surprising joy of the garden at Mottisfont is the collection of old roses that has been assembled in the former kitchen garden. The collection has been made by Graham Thomas and is administered by the National Trust. Here dozens of old shrub roses and species roses scent the air in summer.

Ness Gardens, Wirral, Cheshire (University of Liverpool Botanic Garden)

Perched on the Wirral peninsula, overlooking the estuary of the river Dee and sloping towards the south, the gardens at Ness benefit from the moist south-west air currents which fall over the hills of North Wales. Originally the garden belonged to A. K. Bulley, a patron of plant collecting at the beginning of the twentieth century.

The whole area at Ness is richly planted and there are collections of rhododendrons and azaleas, roses, shrubs, a marvellous double-sided herbaceous border, a woodland garden, a heather garden, a water garden and a remarkably fine rock garden. Each visitor will have his favourite section; all are very well maintained and spacious. Perhaps the rock garden is the most enjoyable. It is spacious, scaling the slope above the water garden, and is well sheltered by trees. While there is much mixed planting there, there are also some alpine treasures to be seen. The main terrace above it provides a microclimate for a number of shrubs generally regarded as doubtfully hardy and there are beds in front of the wall, maintained in colourful planting with begonias and other splendid bedding plants.

The shrub collection provides interest at all seasons, and many of the plants have been purchased with funds provided by the Friends of Ness. The care and interest that is lavished upon this garden shows in every department.

Nymans, Handcross, near Crawley, West Sussex

Nymans is a garden to enjoy for its immense range of plants and planting ideas and for its naturalness. It is renowned especially for its collections of flowering trees and shrubs such as magnolias, rhododendrons, camellias and euchryphias. *Euchryphia nymansensis* originated in this garden.

The original house was destroyed by fire but remarkably some of the tender plants that were growing on the walls survived, so the ruin now forms a picturesque backdrop to the garden and supports numerous interesting plants. The forecourt near the present house is formal in concept and at one side of the house is a walled garden containing some unusual flowering trees and many shrubs and perennials; a stone dovecote has been built into the wall. At the centre, where the paths meet, is a simple small Italian fountain, and clipped yews shaped as a ball and casket stand around it.

It is not so much the design of the garden as the plants that absorb the visitor's attention and apart from the flowering trees and shrubs there are good herbaceous plants. The borders were originally designed by William Robinson and are decorated with clipped yews. In spring, when the trees are in flower, the ground is carpeted with naturalised bulbs, mainly daffodils. At the end of the garden is a good pinetum where numerous unusual conifers are to be found, many of them collected at the end of the nineteenth century.

Packwood House, Hockley Heath, Warwickshire

The garden at Packwood House is arranged in two separate areas, both relatively simple but quite dramatic. Nearer the house is a seventeenth-century garden walled around in pink brick prettily decorated with plants. There are four pavilions, one at each corner. Decorative brickwork and round windows enhance the pavilions, which are not of the same age. Two house the fireplaces used for heating the walls when fruit was grown upon them.

The second garden lies beyond and is reached by semicircular brick steps and a gate in the wall. The visitor should turn at the foot of these steps to see the scooped arches at the base of the wall. These were designed to house lipwork beehives and are called bee boles. The arresting topiary that stands ahead is known as 'The Sermon on the Mount'. The clipped specimens are thought to represent the Master, the apostles and the multitude. The lawn rises to the mount, which was probably there before the planting of the trees, most of which are believed to have been planted in the nineteenth century.

Polesden Lacey, near Dorking, Surrey

The formality of the garden at Polesden Lacey belies the natural contour of the land, for the site appears to form a valley running east-west, with the house perched above it. The delight is in the planting in a series of separate gardens, enclosed and complete in themselves. Little secluded corners with an ornament, seat or just a bowl add an intimacy that lingers about the whole scheme. One garden is planted entirely of lavender, the flint wall around it decorated with aubretia dotted all over it. Another garden is of roses, another of irises, and so on. The flowery profusion never becomes overpowering because stark clipped yew hedges dominate the terrace which runs across the valley. The battlement-like pattern of the hedges provides a good backdrop for statuary and also allows glimpses of other parts of the garden.

Powis Castle, Welshpool, Powys

The pink sandstone castle at Powis dominates a steep slope on which a virtual hanging garden has been made. Looking up from below towards the castle the pattern emerges, formed by deep terraces and topped by enormous clipped Irish yews. The dome shape into which they have been cut is echoed on the second terrace by the archways of a brick loggia — thought to have been an aviary because the terrace is called Aviary Terrace. Each terrace is of a different depth and breadth. The third juts well forward and an orangery is built into the wall. Balustrading forms a pattern along this terrace and along the approach steps at the side of the scaling edifice. Much of the balustrading is decorated with lead figures of shepherds and shepherdesses and elsewhere on the terracing and walls are great urns. Climbing up to the terraces, the visitor has a superb view over the Breiddon Hills and then sees that below there is a huge formal garden broken up by high clipped hedges. A double hedge runs across the whole of the area. To one side is the old kitchen garden as well as a formal lawn with circular pool and more clipped trees. The terraces mainly harbour the good planting because they are frost free, the cold air draining downwards. Trees are important at Powis, because not only are they planted in the garden but there is a good pinetum as well. Beyond the garden proper, and beyond the control of the National Trust, is Gwen Morgan's Wood, where there are some very good trees, especially conifers and one notable Douglas fir, *Pseudostuga menziesii,* over 180 feet (55 m) in height.

Pusey House, near Faringdon, Oxfordshire

This a delightfully English garden, formally designed near the house and trailing into informality around the lake. In the sheltered flower garden near the house — known as Lady Emily's Garden and almost a secret garden behind a wall — there are many flowering perennials and climbers on the walls. From the gate of this garden the visitor can wander either towards a temple and woodland area and along the far bank of the lake or turn in the opposite direction towards the terrace and the house. This is paved and dotted with cushion plants and plants in containers to add seasonal colour. Further on among shrubs is a striking orange border of day lilies, alchemilla and euphorbias, and further still the path winds towards the Chinese bridge. From almost every part of the garden this long wooden bridge, painted white, can be seen crossing the lake at its narrow part. Waterlilies and other bog-loving plants abound along the margins of the lake hereabouts. The level site allows many extensive views of the garden and everywhere delightful planting and combinations of planting material will interest the visitor.

Rousham House, Steeple Aston, Oxfordshire

Rousham was one of the first eighteenth-century landscape gardens to be made and it needs some interpretation to be enjoyed. Behind the house and level bowling green the land falls away and as one descends the woodland path the man-made landscape garden is slowly revealed, much smaller than the usual surviving eighteenth-century landscape gardens. William Kent began this garden at Rousham in the first half of the eighteenth century and there have been additions since, some of them in Kent's lifetime, but the theme is one of greenery and buildings and informal glades and statuary.

As one approaches the slope to descend a view over a balustrade of the bend in the river Cherwell suggests the informality to come. Below the balustrading the path leads to an arcade known as Praeneste (note the seats specially designed by Kent for his building) and beyond to the left lies the classical dream garden: grassy glades, Venus's Vale — a rising piece of ground with cascades and a formal pool, called the Great Pool — and woodland walks leading to temples and more statuary. A narrow serpentine water conduit leads to the bath house, or Cold Bath, and small pool. Its wavering course may not appear strange today, but after the formality and rigidity of the sixteenth and seventeenth centuries it must have been one of the first uses of the serpentine form.

The bend in the river enfolds the garden and the old thirteenth-century bridge over the Cherwell forms part of the landscape.

Climbing back and past the house the visitor comes to the former kitchen garden, now decked with roses and herbaceous perennials as well as old fruit trees. Beyond that a small old-world rose garden is tucked away behind the stable block and in the middle is a round dovecote. This little complex is a good example of what a domestic estate and home farm comprised in former centuries.

St Fagan's Castle, near Cardiff, South Glamorgan

The garden that surrounds the Welsh Folk Museum, Amgueddfa Werin Cymru, at St Fagan's Castle is old in both design and content. The hanging garden scaling the slope is terraced, each level decorated with nineteenth-century balustrading. The garden below offers one surprise after another: two pleached lime walks, a hornbeam arbour, very good old plane trees, and colourful bedding carried out in the knot-garden style. Perhaps the most remarkable feature is a walled garden in which there is a mulberry orchard. The mulberry tree *(Morus niger)* was introduced into Britain in 1500 and was grown far more in the past than it is today.

Savill Garden and Valley Garden, Windsor Great Park, near Englefield Green, Surrey

At the southern end of Windsor Great Park the Savill Garden and the Valley Garden have been made since the 1930s under the care of Sir Eric Savill. Progress was halted by the Second World War but development has continued since then, especially in the making of the Valley Garden, so that today they are remarkably fine gardens.

Essentially a woodland garden that runs alongside a stream and bog area, the Savill Garden is famous for meconopsis, cardiocrinums, rodgersias and lilies, all of which are planted in the glades. In the wet areas and margins of the stream great patches of gunnera, lysichitum and primulas soften the water's edge. Glades open out to a level garden planted mainly with climbing and bush roses, and further towards the wild woodland area there is a small formal rose garden. There is a long double herbaceous border where there is mixed planting with some unusual shrubs, and beyond this an old wall backs on to a sheltered area where a microclimate has been formed to harbour tender wall plants. Raised beds run along this area, each bed filled with a different soil so that a wide range of plants can be grown.

A stretch of woodland further to the south has become known as the Valley Garden. Azaleas are the salient feature here in late spring, especially in an area called the Punch Bowl, and earlier daffodils in thousands flower under the trees throughout the gardens. Sheets of colour spill down the slopes in early summer. This woodland area has been tamed in such a way that heathers and hydrangeas seem to be growing naturally and not to have been planted.

These two gardens are probably the best examples of the twentieth-century wild garden, with restrained planting setting just the right key.

Sezincote, near Moreton-in-Marsh, Gloucestershire

The Indianesque style of the house at Sezincote is followed through in the garden and it is refreshing to find this variation. The curving arm of the house is a conservatory or corridor. It helps to enfold a lawn which is slit by a narrow canal bordered by equally slim cypresses. Elsewhere in this part of the garden is a little Indian pavilion.

Behind the house the land forms a small ravine which has been cleverly fashioned as a rock garden with a tumbling stream falling down it. Much lush greenery of ferns, aruncus and gunnera clothes the rocks and the stream side. Crossing the ravine is a bridge also of Indianesque style and above it are a circular pool and fountain and another little Indian temple with the goddess Souriya. This is a gem of a garden!

Sheffield Park, near Uckfield, East Sussex

In spring or in autumn the woodland at Sheffield Park is a colourful spectacle. Azaleas and rhododendrons provide the main bold splashes of colour early in the year, but the garden is best known for its autumn colour. This is produced by splendid trees and shrubs such as beeches, parrotias and nyssas and perhaps most splendidly by *Taxodium distichum* reflected in the lake. Sheffield Park is a twentieth-century collection of trees and shrubs, with some underplanting, all put within a former landscape garden. The original large lake was formed to the design of 'Capability' Brown in the eighteenth century and a hundred years later the two smaller lakes were formed and the rock cascade was contrived to join them to control water levels. Woodland paths and vistas, the water and the excellent plants make a visit to Sheffield Park well worthwhile both for the scenic enjoyment and for the trees themselves.

Sissinghurst Castle, near Cranbrook, Kent

Well known as the home of the late Vita Sackville-West, who transformed the garden within a plan devised by her husband, Sir Harold Nicolson, Sissinghurst is now under the care of the National Trust. As with many other twentieth-century gardens, it consists of a number of small areas connected and integrated by planting. The overall impression is of cottage-garden luxuriance: roses spill about in summer, good foliage plants soften the lines and the old buildings provide a warm backdrop to the scene, at the same time remaining part of the design. Bulbs and perennial plants abound, the sheltered borders harbour numerous interesting plants and the clipped yew hedges enfold little surprises. A silver or white garden is especially delightful and one comes upon a gold and orange border and then a blue one. The most important of the self-contained gardens is the rose garden, which dominates one's memories of Sissinghurst and has made it a garden renowned for its abounding roses. The formal herb garden with its simple bowl container was one of the earliest to be made and was started before the Second World War.

Sizergh Castle, near Kendal, Cumbria

The National Trust controls the garden at Sizergh Castle, which despite its small size is the mecca of pteridologists — or fern lovers. The ancient castle walls provide shelter for several interesting plants and the formal terrace gives way to a small area of terracing and steps overlooking a lily pool. But at one side of the building there is an attractive rock and water garden and here innumerable species and forms of fern are found growing under ideal conditions. Well disposed foliage plants and colourful small trees such as Japanese maples and compact-growing conifers break up the area so that the paths have to be explored. This rock garden is set in a bowl sheltered by larger trees, so a congenial microclimate exists within this part of the garden. Elsewhere there are lawns and mixed planting.

Spetchley Park, near Worcester, Worcestershire

The Georgian mansion at Spetchley overlooks a landscaped park towards the Malvern Hills. A long pool, part of the old moat which once encircled an Elizabethan house burned down by the Cromwellians after the Battle of Worcester, separates the house and its attendant shrubberies from a far more intimate garden. So there are two gardens at Spetchley Park, almost inconspicuously joined, with the one not intruding upon the other.

The main garden is set in sections, some of them treated quite formally. The walls of the kitchen garden provide splendid sites for borders of hardy perennials and shrubs, well sheltered by yew hedges, and the north wall protects the old melon yard. In the centre of one of these borders there is a loggia and a central grassy pathway bordered by clipped hedges leads from it to a series of rectangular formal gardens opening off this central axis. Then the garden opens out into lawn and shrub planting, on the one hand connecting it to the landscape garden and leading to an area planted with acers near the lake path, and on the other hand leading to a curious old thatched summerhouse and a splendid iron shelter with a glass roof. Here an arrangement of container-grown plants is assembled and ivies entwine the central pillars.

Stourhead, near Mere, Wiltshire

Stourhead was one of the first of the great landscape gardens created in the eighteenth century when English taste broke away from the rigidity of design of the sixteenth and seventeenth centuries, and it is now one of the best-known. A valley with ponds was flooded to form a lake and a circuitous walk was made along the banks, carefully contrived to afford changing views of the surroundings and to concentrate the attention inwards towards the garden. Several buildings of fine design were erected at vantage points along the walk. Classical temples to Apollo and to Flora, a Pantheon and a rustic or 'Gothic' cottage are all placed to entice the walker and enhance the landscape. The enjoyment of classicism was a fashionable cult conjunctive to the landscape movement in general and the garden of Stourhead was made quite apart from the house to which it belonged. To one side of the lake there is a man-made grotto, where the *River God* reigns (see page 18), and through the arches there is an intended view of the Temple of Flora on the opposite bank of the lake.

The simplicity of the original design has been blurred by subsequent tree planting and the National Trust continues a sound policy of tree replacement. Conifers, introduced into

Britain mainly in the nineteenth century, are now a feature of the planting and rhododendrons also are more recent than the original landscape.

Stowe, near Buckingham, Buckinghamshire

The immense scale of the landscape garden at Stowe may fail in its impact for many visitors at first, because it lacks the grandeur of Castle Howard, for example, or the compactness of Rousham. The surrounding countryside appears not to play an integral part. But if the circuitous walk is taken as advised in the guide a series of related landscapes will be seen, several lovely buildings and a great central open area which, in reality, is a wide vista from the building behind (now a boys' school) to the lake and twin pavilions forward, and beyond to an enormous Corinthian arch.

Perhaps the most exciting part of the garden, at all times of the year, is the Elysian Fields, to the south-east of the building. But go in late winter or early spring before the foliage obliterates the view and before the grass has lengthened to obscure the contours of the land. When only the bird song intrudes, the valley is well named 'Elysian Fields'. William Kent formed this valley in 1735, trying to emulate some sort of classical wilderness. On the west bank is the Temple of Virtue, considered to be Kent's best garden temple (c. 1734), with a circular colonnade from which one can look down across the water called Worthies River (or Styx) upon the Temple of British Worthies. Also by Kent, the alcoves of the Temple accommodate busts of such worthies as Elizabeth I, Shakespeare, Bacon, Milton and William III, sculptured by Rysbrack and Scheemakers.

Over towards the eastern extremity of the garden at this point the Palladian Bridge crosses the head of the Octagonal lake, ather lost in reeds at some seasons. There are three such bridges in England, at Wilton, which was the first, at Prior Park, Bath, and this one at Stowe. The two latter are copies of that at Wilton, which was built in 1737. A walk curves back, crossing under the archway of the bridge, and along the south bank of the lake, passing the Temple of Friendship by Gibb and then the pebble alcove (see page 11) and two pavilions on the same axis as the south portico of the house and the Corinthian Arch. By walking towards the house to the Rotundo, designed by Vanbrugh in 1721, one reaches the focal point of the whole vast expanse of Stowe. Radiating views across open parkland to various eyecatchers emphasise the immensity and near desolation of this landscape.

Studley Royal, near Ripon, North Yorkshire

The landscape garden at Studley Royal was started between 1715 and 1720 by John Aislabie as a romantic scenic composition. The river Skell was formed into a series of pools, canals and formal ponds and the banks of the river were planted. The towering wooded cliffs provided the complete introspective seclusion required.

Much later, in about 1768, the family was able to acquire Fountains Abbey, a romantic ruin, beyond the stretch of the river, to provide the perfect culmination of the vista along the meandering river. The visitor can be so enchanted by the enclosed design that he may not realise that the pools are formal within the natural setting of the craggy valley. The classical temple in Palladian style on the bank opposite the main walk is believed to be the work of Colin Campbell and was restored recently. On the hilltop beyond the formal pools there is a vantage point from which one can look down upon the smooth course of the river towards the ruined abbey, so much a part of the romanticism of the whole concept.

Tatton Park, near Knutsford, Cheshire

The park surrounding this garden was landscaped by Humphry Repton at the end of the eighteenth century but is now relatively unimportant to the garden visitor to Tatton Park. The gardens have been added to periodically over the years and there are now several differing styles of garden and a number of interesting buildings under the administration of the National Trust.

The main facade of the house overlooks a sunken Victorian parterre with a pool and fountain at the centre and a stone balustrade running across the width of the garden, designed by Sir Joseph Paxton. Also near the house, but to one side of it, are an orangery, an aviary and plant houses, the most impressive of which is a fernery. This was established about 1850 to house a collection introduced from New Zealand, and numerous tender ferns still flourish there. Backing on to this is a wall, which runs behind an L-shaped herbaceous border where there is some pleasing mixed planting. The urns which decorate the top of the wall are chimney pots from the flues and hearths contained in the wall. They were formerly used to keep frost away for the successful cultivation of fruit.

The end of the border leads towards a small folly or tower surrounded by a little garden and then the main path runs southward towards the site of a former monument, badly damaged by subsidence, and passes the lake to the right. Here on an island there is a Shinto temple. Beyond that is the Japanese garden, which was made early in the twentieth century. Walks around the pool, or the Golden Brook as it is called, are planted with rhododendrons, azaleas and maples and lead to a pinetum and scattered trees under which many spring flowering bulbs are planted, particularly bluebells. Returning eastwards and then to the house, the visitor sees small buildings and shrub planting, a beech maze and then a small pool with a statue of Mercury in the centre. Tatton Park is a garden to wander in.

Tintinhull, near Yeovil, Somerset

The garden at Tintinhull is one of the most recently made in Britain, having been started just before the Second World War. It is formal in concept and separate compartments have been formed and are connected by terracing set at shallow but varying levels. On entering, the visitor sees the Cedar Lawn, surrounded by borders of mixed planting with roses, herbs, peonies, lilac, magnolias, clematis and a wide variety of hardy herbaceous perennials. Beyond lies the pool garden, where a long rectangular lily pool is set in the grass with a summerhouse at its head. There is always a good variety of plants in containers scattered about this portico. There are containers on the terraces too, where agapanthus are cultivated in huge pots. To one side and in front of the house is the azalea garden, rich in colour in the spring, and a central path leads across Eagle Court, where on either side clipped box bushes resembling great cushions add an unexpectedly prim air to what is otherwise a flower garden. The path is centred on the house and extends to a tiny parterre and lily pool. To one side is an enormous ilex, but everywhere there are excellent planting ideas and examples of the right use of plants. Generous mixed planting is the keynote of Tintinhull, a small garden belonging to the National Trust. At each season of the year there are good and effectively disposed plants to be found.

Trengwainton, near Penzance, Cornwall

West Cornwall has a very mild climate allowing numerous exotic plants to be grown successfully. Trengwainton is perhaps the most interesting of several gardens in the area, even to the plantsman, for the breadth of its collection. The layout of the garden also is attractive; two main areas are linked by a long drive along which runs a stream. The bank is richly planted with trees, shrubs and herbaceous perennials as well as bog-loving plants. The first section of the garden reached by the visitor consists of a series of bays in which plants are thoroughly sheltered. Then the drive runs towards the house where the landscaping is more conventional with lawns and lavish rhododendron planting.

Other gardens to be seen in west Cornwall are Trelissick and Trewithen, both near Truro and both of much interest in spring for the enormous rhododendrons, collections of flowering trees and numerous tender plants, many of them introduced in the late nineteenth century and early twentieth century.

Tudor House Museum Garden, Southampton, Hampshire

Behind the Tudor House Museum in Bugle Street, South-
ampton, lies a small but fascinating garden. It is faithfully
reconstructed as a sixteenth-century garden, filled with herbs
and simple plants known in Tudor times. At the centre is a knot
garden of clipped close planted herbs, surrounded by formal
beds. Each plant is labelled with its Latin and English names, its
provenance and economic use. Arbours with climbing plants
growing up them, heraldic beasts and elm rails have all been
accurately designed to fit into the period detail. There is a little
water conduit because every early garden had its source of
water. Gardens of the period, visited by a number of people,
always had a privy garden exclusive to the residents. So, on
entering, this secret garden can be glimpsed through the
enfolding bay hedge. Although small, this garden is well worth a
detour to visit.

Waddesdon Manor, near Aylesbury, Buckinghamshire

The park at Waddesdon Manor, with many fine trees,
surrounds a conical hill on which a flat plateau was formed in the
nineteenth century for the house. The drive curls around the
hillside through a deer park and rich evergreen planting, but the
garden immediately surrounding the house is formal and there is
French, Italian and Dutch statuary. On the south terrace, from
which there is a distant view over the Vale of Aylesbury, is a
formal parterre with an impressive central basin and lead fountain
in the Italian manner, and bedding plants add colour at each side.
The parterre is surrounded by hedges and stone balustrading;
flights of shallow steps regulate the fall of the slope as the garden
extends to further lawns dotted with huge trees and runs into the
park beyond. To the west of the house is a unique aviary garden, in
which the National Trust has planted the rose 'Iceberg' to emphasise the white central chamber of the aviary, where there is
statuary and a fountain of marble. The aviary houses very many
interesting birds, and colourful macaws fly free in the surrounding
area. The treillage pavilions of the aviary form a splendid building
in themselves. Statues of birds and animals decorate the lawns and
the whole area of this garden is delightfully relaxed amid the
sophistication of the remainder of the garden at Waddesdon. In
front of the mansion, which is of French Renaissance style, is a
very wide level area uncluttered by planting or statuary; to one
side, beyond the slope, a somewhat sombre rock garden has been
formed of large boulders.

Wallington, Cambo, Northumberland

There is a garden surrounding the house at Wallington but the
main attraction for the visitor is a walled garden reached by a

woodland walk. Within the formal confines of a wall a terrace has been built up at one side with buildings and overlooks a delightful informal garden consisting of lawn and flower beds with some rock work, in and out of which a stream meanders. Its course is entertaining, for it disappears underground at points, to reappear a little further on. The terrace itself is bedecked with roses and other shrubs and immediately below flowering trees are dotted about, each within its own pool of flowers. On the terrace are a large conservatory and greenhouses and of special interest is the collection of fuchsias, some of them very old. Wallington belongs to the National Trust.

Westbury Court, Westbury-on-Severn, Gloucestershire

One of the very few remaining examples of seventeenth-century water gardens made in the Dutch style is at Westbury. It was perhaps the first to be made in England. The National Trust during the 1970s has restored the garden to its former simple splendour. The design is very straightforward and much of it can be seen from the road (A48). It consists of two formal canals. One is quite straight with a Dutch pavilion at its head; the other is T-shaped, wider and with a statue of the god Neptune. A clipped yew hedge surrounds the water. The National Trust renovated this hedge and found that the water works were repairable. The pavilion has been rebuilt working from the original plans and accounts, so that what is seen today at Westbury is a close representation of seventeenth-century style. The original house was demolished some time ago; the present building is an old persons' home but it does not detract from the scheme and is behind the wall.

Nearby there is another formal water garden made at the same time and in the same simple style. It is at Frampton Court.

West Wycombe Park, near High Wycombe, Buckinghamshire

The landscaped park at West Wycombe lies across a valley of the Chilterns with the river Wye flowing through it. It was made during the eighteenth century, mainly by the owner, Sir Francis Dashwood, with the help of professional landscapists. Today the rolling hillside remains much the same. Amid the lake formed by the damming of the river and known as Swan Lake is an island where there is an elegant Music Temple. There is a cascade and nearby there are caves for the visitor to explore and a mausoleum up on the hill.

Wilton House, Wilton, Wiltshire

Most gardeners know of the famous cedars of Lebanon at Wilton House. Some were planted only in the first decade of the twentieth century; others are thought to be very much older —

some are even claimed as seventeenth-century plants, which would have been there before the formal gardens of the period were cleared away for the landscaping that followed. Perhaps the outstanding feature at Wilton is the smooth level lawn, surrounded by and dotted with lovely tree planting, including many limes, planes and oaks. At one side the river Nadder flows through water meadows and is crossed by the dramatic Palladian bridge, designed by Roger Morris for the Earl of Pembroke in 1737.

Under the walls of the building are beds of mixed planting and climbers. Behind the house, and not open to the public, is an Italian-style garden. This may be seen at a distance to be formal in concept, with terracing, statuary and balustrades.

The past glories of Wilton can only be imagined from drawings, but it was one of the earliest grand gardens in England. Today in the entrance forecourt is one of the most imaginative projects of garden architecture of the present day. Designed by David Vicary in 1971, it is a formal garden with fine jet fountains, which reflect light on the darkest of days, surrounded by limes and underplanted in lavenders and pinks. So much does the design appear to be part of the scene that unobservant visitors have been known to overlook it — surely evidence of its suitability to its surroundings.

Wisley, near Ripley, Surrey (The Royal Horticultural Society's Garden)

The garden at Wisley was made at the very beginning of the twentieth century, when natural and woodland planting — or wild gardening as it came to be called — was the latest idea. Today the vast range of plants to be seen there provides some interest for every gardener, however sophisticated or simple his requirement might be. There are acres of tree and shrub planting away from the main garden along by the river Wey, and a pinetum links this area with the main garden, which is the part most visitors know. There are also a heather garden, lakes, island beds, various plant collections such as ferns and grasses, herbaceous borders, a rose garden, a rock and water garden, a herb and aromatic garden, glasshouses, a formal water garden and a wide area of rhododendron and azalea planting, known as Battleston Hill, for which Wisley is justly famous.

Wrest Park, Silsoe, Bedfordshire

In the garden at Wrest Park the garden historian can see a clear variety of period styles. It has been added to by a series of owners, rather than remodelled, and so presents an interesting exercise.

The terrace behind the house overlooks an immense parterre in the French manner. Statuary and clipped Portugal laurels line the central pathway, which is on the same axis as a long canal of water far beyond. At the far end of the canal, seemingly as far as the eye can see, is a delightful pavilion, built by Thomas Archer. From an upper floor a splendid view of the layout of the garden can be seen. At each side thickly planted woodland or *bosquet* is cut through by a complex of *allées,* decorated by statuary and urns in the French manner. Of the garden buildings the Bowling Green House and the orangery by Clephane are the best and are situated to one side between the parterre and the canal. In this part of the garden also there is a rustic eighteenth-century bath house from which emanates a source of water, persuaded into a mock river by 'Capability' Brown. This river curves away, washing the boundary of the woodland in a most natural way. Near the house there is some good planting in a mixed border backed by the wall of the old kitchen garden.

Rousham House, Oxfordshire.

Glossary

Allée, Alley: there is a subtle difference between the French *allée*, which is a straight pathway or ride cut through thickly planted woodland, and the English *alley*, which is usually applied to path between high hedges or buildings.

Arboretum: a collection of trees, both evergreen and deciduous, usually planted as specimens.

Bedding: close planting in formal manner to make patterns or colour combinations of plants raised elsewhere. Seen most commonly in suburban gardens, northern public parks and in some large parterres in spring and summer.

Chinoiserie: the name given to a style fashionable during the whole of the eighteenth century — a counterfeit form of Chinese taste. The pagoda at Kew is an example.

Dutch garden: a formal style of garden, incorporating clipped plants on geometric lines (perhaps topiary) and enclosed water in formal basins.

Formal garden: a site in which some symmetry of design is detectable, be it elaborate as in a parterre or simple as in a rectangular lily pool sited in a lawn. Often a formal garden is constructed upon a level site or a series of level sites incorporating terraces, steps and walling.

French-style garden: elaborate layouts rigid in conception, influenced by French taste in the seventeenth century. Good use is usually made of water, as fountains, and of statuary.

Gazebo: a small building, usually of two storeys, set at some vantage point in the garden for watching the approaches or the surrounding countryside.

Grotto: an eighteenth-century foible, grotto making resulted in a collection of stones to form 'houses', ravines, caves and tunnels. Frequently the buildings were lined with bones, fossils or attractive pebbles, or decorated with shells.

Ha-ha: a ditch invisible from the garden, constructed to prevent entry and avoiding the building of a fence which would impair the view. In section it is a ditch with one side upright (estate side), faced with stones or bricks, and the other side sloping (park or common land side). It also prevents cattle from entering the garden.

Informal garden: the term did not exist before the eighteenth century when all gardens were constructed on formal and rigid lines. A plan devoid of formality — a garden designed to look natural like a woodland garden *(q.v.)* or beds set out in a seemingly haphazard manner.

Italianate garden: a garden designed in the Italian style of terraces, balustrades, stairways and statuary, all within formal lines. The best Italianate garden in Britain is at Shrubland Hall (Suffolk) but is unfortunately not often open to the public.

Parterre: a symmetrical, formally designed area of considerable proportion intended to be looked upon from above so that the whole pattern can be enjoyed. The site is level and often sub-divided symmetrically into beds, each patterned within itself.

Pergola: a structure for the support of climbing plants. Most frequently seen as a continuous archway or arcade over a path-way, but also to be seen as a screen or patio cover.

Pinetum: a collection of conifers, or cone-bearing trees.

Rustic work: the employment of barked wood in forming trellises, pergolas, summerhouses, seats, etc; usually comparatively short-lived structures, and liable to harbour garden pests. The style is sometimes copied in cast iron — in former years — or in plastic.

Sunken garden: an area, usually comparatively small, constructed at a lower level than the surrounding garden.

Terrace: a raised level space, in garden architecture usually running along a wall of a house or the retaining wall of a higher terrace. Terracing is a method of traversing a steep slope and at the same time retaining level walking areas.

Topiary: the practice of clipping evergreens into geometrical and other forms.

Treillage: an elaborate trellis, with some additional and non-functional ornament.

Water garden: a garden in which water is featured in either formal or informal confines, or as fountains, cascades or spouts.

Wild garden: an informal planting of trees and shrubs with underplanting of shade-loving plants and naturalised bulbs. A type of gardening advocated by William Robinson and only popular since the beginning of the present century.

Woodland garden: a plantation of trees and shrubs emulating a woodland. The plants themselves are often of great interest, flowering trees or a shrub collection underplanted with bulbs.

Index

INDEX